48 LAWS OF INFLUENCE

Mastering the Art of Persuasion and Power

Norris Elliott

NORRIS ELLIOTT BOOKS/ELLIONAIRE BOOKS

Dedication

*To those who seek to understand and master the art
of influence, This book is dedicated to the leaders,
communicators, and change-makers who strive to make a
positive impact on the world. May these principles guide
you in your journey to inspire, persuade, and connect with
others, fostering a world built on trust, understanding, and
mutual respect. To my family and friends, whose support
and encouragement have been the foundation of my
endeavors, And to all the mentors and thinkers who have
shared their wisdom and insights, shaping my understanding
of the intricate dance of influence. This book is for you.*

Epigraph

"Influence is not about convincing others to see the world as you do; it's about seeing the world as they do and guiding them gently towards a new perspective." Unknown

ELLIONAIRE

CONTENTS

WELCOME

Dear Reader,

Thank you for choosing "The 48 Laws of Influence: Mastering the Art of Persuasion and Power." Your decision to embark on this journey of understanding and mastering influence is a testament to your commitment to personal and professional growth.

We are thrilled to share with you the insights and strategies that can transform the way you communicate and lead. Each chapter is designed to equip you with the tools necessary to inspire, persuade, and connect with those around you, fostering meaningful and lasting relationships.

Your feedback is invaluable to us. If you find this book helpful, we would greatly appreciate it if you could take a moment to leave a review on Amazon. Your reviews not only help us understand how we can better serve you but also assist other readers in discovering the benefits of this book.

We invite you to join our email list for updates, exclusive content, and special offers. By signing up, you'll receive:

- Notifications about new book releases
- Exclusive insights and tips on influence and persuasion
- Invitations to webinars and events
- Special promotions and discounts

To join our email list, simply send an email to ellionairebooks@gmail.com with the subject line "Subscribe." We look forward to staying connected and continuing to support your journey in mastering the art of influence.

Thank you once again for your support. We wish you great success on your journey to mastering the art of influence.

Warm regards,

Norris Elliott

INTRODUCTION

In a realm where influence is the ultimate currency, the mastery of persuasion becomes the key to unlocking monumental personal and professional success. "The 48 Laws of Influence: Mastering the Art of Persuasion and Power" is meticulously crafted as a comprehensive guide, offering a profound arsenal of strategies that enhance your ability to sway, motivate, and shape outcomes to your advantage.

Each law in this book distills powerful insights drawn from the broad annals of social psychology, evolutionary biology, and historical successes and failures. Here, influence is portrayed not as an innate gift, but as a precise art and science that can be learned and mastered by those who are willing to delve deep into its practices. Each chapter unveils a principle of persuasion that has been instrumental in human interactions, driving the dynamics of relationships, businesses, and even the fate of nations.

Why do we delve into these laws? Because life itself is a grand stage of strategy and interaction. Every decision we make, every relationship we nurture, and every goal we pursue involves subtle plays of influence and persuasion. To navigate this complex arena with finesse, we need more than raw desire; we need tactical acumen. The 48 laws provided in this book equip you with that necessary strategy, enabling a refined approach to influencing thoughts, behaviors, and decisions.

As you explore this book, you will encounter laws such as the Law of Reciprocity, which sheds light on the transformative power of exchange and the undercurrents that govern acts of giving and receiving. You will master the Law of Scarcity, discovering why things rare are perceived as extraordinary.

You will apply the Law of Authority, crafting your presence in ways that naturally draw respect and compliance. From understanding the nuanced power of the Law of Silence to harnessing the assertive essence of the Law of Power, each law is a stepping stone to building a comprehensive blueprint for effective influence.

This text is not a promise of immediate triumph or effortless mastery. The art of influence demands patience, persistence, and a deep engagement with its principles. However, for those who are committed to understanding and applying these strategies, the rewards can be transformative. Whether your aim is to ascend in your career, enhance your interpersonal relationships, or assert greater control over your destiny, these laws pave a path not just to superior strategies but to profound insights.

Prepare to see the world of interaction differently as you turn each page. Prepare to rethink how you communicate, negotiate, and convince. Above all, prepare for transformation, for through the mastery of these laws, you will not only change how others perceive you but also how you perceive the world. Welcome to your journey into the essence of influence, a journey that will redefine your potential and expand the horizons of your influence.

CHAPTER 1: THE LAW OF RECIPROCITY

Understanding Reciprocity

At the heart of human interaction lies the Law of Reciprocy, a powerful principle that drives our social exchanges. The concept is simple yet profound: when someone does something for us, we feel compelled to return the favor. This reflex is not merely cultural; it is wired into our psychology, forming the backbone of societies by promoting mutual support and cooperation.

The Psychological Basis

Research in social psychology suggests that reciprocity is rooted in our evolutionary history. It has helped our ancestors survive by fostering group cohesion and mutual aid. When we receive a favor, our brain triggers a sense of indebtedness, creating a social obligation to reciprocate. This is not just a social nicety but a compelling force, often leading us to return favors disproportionately larger than what we received.

Applications in Everyday Life

Everyday interactions are rife with examples of reciprocity. Consider a simple act of a neighbor bringing you a meal when you are ill. Instinctively, you might feel the need to return the favor, perhaps by helping them with a chore in the future. This unspoken exchange strengthens bonds and builds trust within the community.

Reciprocity in Business

In the business world, recipropty can be a strategic tool. Companies often provide free samples, knowing that many consumers will feel an implicit pressure to purchase more products. Similarly, corporate gifts to clients can renew contracts or facilitate negotiations, as these gestures create a sense of personal connection and indebtedness.

Leveraging Reciprocity

To effectively use reciprocity in persuasion, it is crucial to understand its nuances:

1. **The Initiation**: The act of giving first is crucial. It sets the tone and establishes the giver as generous and caring, qualities that naturally attract reciprocity.

2. **Value of the Gift**: The perceived value of what is given significantly impacts the urge to reciprocate. The gift need not be expensive; even small, thoughtful gestures can trigger a strong reciprocal response.

3. **Timing and Relevance**: The timing and relevance of the gift enhance its effectiveness. Offering something that the recipient needs at the moment can magnify the sense of indebtedness and the resulting reciprocation.

4. **Sincerity**: People discern between genuine acts of kindness and manipulative tactics. Sincerity in the gesture ensures that the act of giving is received as intended, thereby fostering genuine goodwill and cooperation.

Cultural Variations

It's important to recognize that the norms of reciprocity can vary by culture. In some cultures, immediate reciprocation is seen as a way to quickly discharge one's debt, whereas, in others, a delayed response may be more appropriate. Understanding these cultural nuances is crucial when applying reciprocity across different global contexts.

Ethical Considerations

While reciprocity is a potent tool in influence and persuasion, it carries ethical implications. It must be used responsibly, with a clear understanding of the fine line between influencing and manipulating. The best practitioners of reciprocity are those who use it to create positive, mutually beneficial outcomes rather than to take unilateral advantage.

Conclusion

The Law of Reciprocity is a fundamental principle that, when understood and applied with insight and ethical consideration, can significantly enhance your ability to influence and persuade. By engaging in thoughtful acts of giving, you not only foster cooperation and mutual benefit but also build a foundation of trust and respect that can support long-term relationships and collaborations.

CHAPTER 2: THE LAW OF COMMITMENT

The Power of Small Beginnings

The Law of Commitment leverages the human desire to appear consistent in thoughts, words, and actions. Once we commit to something, even in a small way, we are more inclined to go through with larger commitments that align with our initial decision. This psychological principle is powerful because consistency is both a social norm and a personal attribute that people value highly in themselves and others.

Understanding Commitment and Consistency

Commitment triggers one of the most potent psychological processes. When someone commits, either publicly or privately, they align their self-image with that commitment, which makes them more likely to follow through to maintain their self-respect and the respect of others. The consistency principle then comes into play, driving individuals to fulfill commitments to align their future behavior with past actions.

Strategic Applications

1. **Incremental Commitment**: Start by asking for small, non-threatening commitments. For instance, a retailer might ask customers to sign up for a free newsletter rather than make a purchase. Once customers commit to the newsletter, they're more likely to buy products later because they see themselves as interested customers.

2. **Public Commitments**: When people express commitments publicly, they are significantly more likely to follow through.

Public commitments can be facilitated through social media shares, public pledges, or group discussions, which increase the psychological need to maintain consistency.

3. **Written Commitments**: Writing something down increases the commitment level. Businesses often use contracts, written statements, and signed petitions because these documents increase the likelihood that people will stick to their agreements.

The Role of Consistency

Consistency serves as a social and cognitive shortcut. It reduces the complexity of decision-making by allowing us to act in ways that conform to our previous decisions, thereby simplifying our lives and interactions. People perceive consistent behavior as an indicator of trustworthiness and reliability.

Using Commitment to Influence Behavior

1. **Foot-in-the-Door Technique**: This involves securing a small initial commitment that leads to larger commitments. For example, a charity might first ask for a small donation, and once a donor agrees, they may later agree to a more substantial commitment because they now see themselves as supporters of the cause.

2. **Low-Ball Technique**: Initially, offer something at a lower cost or with less effort than will actually be necessary. Once the commitment is made, reveal the true costs. People are likely to stick with their commitment because backing out could lead to inconsistency.

Ethical Implications

While these strategies are effective, they must be used ethically. Manipulating people into commitments they would otherwise avoid can lead to negative outcomes and damage relationships. It is crucial to ensure that the commitments people make are voluntary and informed.

Cultural Considerations

Different cultures perceive commitment and consistency differently. In some cultures, the social pressure to appear consistent is very strong, making commitment-based strategies more effective. In others, flexibility and adaptability might be more valued, requiring different approaches.

Conclusion

The Law of Commitment is a potent tool for influencing behavior. By understanding how to foster commitment in ways that encourage consistency, you can enhance your influence and help others make decisions that align with their values and your objectives. When applied thoughtfully and ethically, this law can lead to beneficial outcomes for all parties involved.

CHAPTER 3: THE LAW OF SOCIAL PROOF

The Essence of Social Proof

Social proof is a psychological phenomenon where people mimic the actions of others in an attempt to reflect correct behavior for a given situation. This influential principle is particularly potent when individuals face uncertainty; they look to others around them to decide how to think, feel, and act. The underlying motivation is the belief that if many people are doing something, it must be the right thing to do.

Understanding Social Influence

Humans are inherently social creatures, and our survival has historically been dependent on our ability to operate within groups. This evolutionary trait explains why we are so attuned to the behaviors and approvals of others. Social proof provides a shortcut for decision making—it's easier and often safer to follow the collective wisdom of the crowd than to figure out everything on our own.

Mechanisms of Social Proof

1. **Conformity**: At its core, social proof often manifests as a form of conformity. Individuals conform to fit into a group, driven by the desire to be accepted by others.

2. **Imitation**: People also engage in imitation, copying behaviors they observe in others, particularly those they respect or see as similar to themselves.

3. **Normalization**: Over time, behaviors that are frequently observed become normalized, making them even more likely to be adopted by others.

Applications in Everyday Life

Social proof can be seen in various everyday contexts, from fashion trends to social media behaviors:

- **Product Reviews and Ratings**: Online shopping platforms utilize social proof through user reviews and ratings. Seeing that others have purchased and endorsed a product can significantly influence potential buyers.
- **Social Media Likes and Shares**: Posts that receive a large number of likes or shares are perceived as more valuable or accurate, leading more people to engage with them.

Social Proof in Marketing

Marketers harness the power of social proof by showcasing popular products, testimonials, and endorsements from celebrities or trusted figures:

- **Testimonials**: Sharing customer testimonials can convince potential customers of a product's worth, as they see that others have had positive experiences.
- **Celebrity Endorsements**: When a well-known personality endorses a product, their followers are likely to trust and purchase it due to the credibility the celebrity brings.

Building and Leveraging Social Proof

To effectively use social proof in persuasion, consider these strategies:

- **Showcase Popularity**: Highlight how popular a decision or action is among a relevant group. For instance, informing customers that an item is a best-seller can spur further purchases.
- **Use Visuals to Amplify Impact**: Visual cues such as queues, crowded venues, or pictures of people using a product can enhance the effect of social proof.
- **Segment by Similarity**: People are more influenced by those they perceive to be similar to themselves. Tailoring messages

to reflect the specific demographics of your target audience can increase the efficacy of social proof.

Ethical Considerations

While social proof is a powerful tool, its application raises ethical questions, particularly regarding the authenticity of the influences being created. Manipulating social proof to create false impressions can lead to consumer distrust and harm reputations.

Conclusion

The Law of Social from others is a pervasive force in human behavior. By understanding and ethically applying this principle, you can significantly enhance your persuasive efforts, whether in personal relationships, business, or broader social interactions. Harnessing social proof effectively means not only influencing decisions but also contributing to an environment where informed, authentic choices are made based on a genuine understanding of collective behaviors.

CHAPTER 4: THE LAW OF AUTHORITY

Understanding the Influence of Authority

Authority wields profound influence over behavior. This law hinges on the principle that people are conditioned to follow the lead of credible, knowledgeable experts. Authority can be established through titles, uniforms, education, and perceived experience. When individuals recognize authority, they are more likely to comply, often without questioning the commands or suggestions made.

The Psychology Behind Authority

The psychological roots of authority stem from early socialization processes where individuals learn to obey figures who are seen as capable of leading, teaching, or enforcing rules, such as parents, teachers, and law enforcement. This conditioning carries into adulthood, where authority figures are often followed unquestioningly. This automatic obedience to authority can be both a social glue that keeps communities organized and a potential pitfall when it leads to blind compliance.

Mechanisms of Establishing Authority

1. **Credentials and Titles**: Displaying diplomas, certificates, or titles immediately elevates a person's perceived authority. Professionals in various fields use this to gain trust and respect from the outset.

2. **Uniforms and Symbols**: Uniforms are powerful symbols of authority that can influence behavior significantly. For

instance, people are more likely to follow directions from someone dressed as a police officer than from someone in casual attire.

3. **Expertise and Knowledge**: Demonstrating expertise through informed opinions, thorough explanations, and confident delivery can establish authority in any field. This is often seen in settings like conferences, where speakers are presumed to be experts in their topics.

Applications in Business and Leadership

In business, authority can enhance leadership effectiveness and persuasive communication:

- **Leadership**: Leaders who establish their authority through both their expertise and their ability to connect on a human level are often more successful in motivating their teams.
- **Marketing**: Businesses use authority by having experts endorse products or by highlighting their own expertise and history in the industry to gain consumer trust.

Building and Leveraging Authority

To effectively harness the Law of Authority, consider these strategies:

- **Showcase Expertise**: Regularly share knowledge through blogs, books, podcasts, or speaking engagements. This not only displays expertise but also keeps you top of mind as an authority in your field.
- **Highlight Endorsements**: Use endorsements from other respected figures in your industry to enhance credibility.
- **Be Consistent and Accurate**: Authority is quickly undermined by factual inaccuracies or inconsistent behavior. Maintain a track record of reliability and truthfulness.

Ethical Considerations

With great power comes great responsibility. Authority should be exercised with ethical considerations at the forefront to avoid abuses of power. Leaders must be vigilant not to exploit their influence but instead use it to foster positive outcomes for their followers and organizations.

Cultural Variations

Cultural context can affect perceptions of authority. In some cultures, authority is intertwined with age and tradition, whereas in others, it is more closely associated with innovation and disruption. Understanding these nuances is crucial for effectively applying authority in a globalized world.

Conclusion

The Law of Authority is a cornerstone of effective persuasion. By understanding and cultivating credible authority, you can enhance your influence, making your arguments more persuasive and your leadership more compelling. However, it's essential to use this power judiciously, ensuring that your influence leads to positive and ethical outcomes.

CHAPTER 5: THE LAW OF LIKING

The Influence of Affinity

T he Law of Liking is based on the simple, yet profound insight that people are more inclined to agree with and be influenced by those whom they like. This principle taps into the basic human need for connection and belonging. When we like someone, we are naturally more receptive to their ideas and requests, often because we see them as extensions of our own values and preferences.

Psychological Foundations of Liking

Liking is rooted in several psychological factors:

1. **Similarity**: We tend to like people who are similar to us —whether in terms of interests, beliefs, backgrounds, or even physical appearance. This similarity fosters a sense of connection and understanding.

2. **Compliments**: We are generally more favorable towards those who compliment us. Compliments can be a powerful tool, as they make us feel good about ourselves and create a positive association with the person giving them.

3. **Cooperation**: Engaging in cooperative tasks can increase liking. When we work together with others towards a common goal, it enhances camaraderie and trust.

4. **Familiarity**: Frequent contact with someone typically increases our liking for them. This is due to the mere exposure effect, where repeated exposure to a person or object fosters familiarity and preference.

Applications in Various Contexts

Understanding and leveraging the Law of Liking can be

beneficial in multiple settings:

- **Sales and Marketing**: Salespeople who establish a rapport with potential customers are more likely to close deals. Similarly, marketing campaigns that resonate with the personal experiences and interests of the audience are often more effective.

- **Workplace Dynamics**: Managers who are liked by their teams generally see higher levels of engagement and productivity. Being likable can also facilitate smoother negotiations and collaborations.

- **Personal Relationships**: In personal spheres, liking plays a crucial role in the formation and maintenance of friendships and romantic relationships.

Building and Leveraging Liking

To harness the Law of Liking effectively, consider the following strategies:

1. **Express Genuine Interest**: Show genuine interest in the other person's life, thoughts, and feelings. Active listening and empathy can significantly enhance your likability.

2. **Mirror and Match**: Subtly mimic the body language, speech patterns, and attitudes of others. This mirroring can increase rapport and make interactions feel more natural and engaging.

3. **Find Common Ground**: Actively seek out similarities and shared interests. Highlighting these commonalities can create a stronger bond and increase the likelihood of positive outcomes.

4. **Be Positive and Complimentary**: Maintain a positive demeanor and be generous with sincere compliments. Positivity is contagious and can significantly boost your likability.

Ethical Considerations

While it is powerful to leverage liking, it is important to

do so ethically. Manipulating others by feigning interest or affection can lead to distrust and damage relationships. Genuine interactions based on authentic mutual respect and interest are not only more ethical but also more sustainable.

Conclusion

The Law of Liking underscores the importance of personal relationships in influencing decisions. By understanding and applying this law with sincerity and ethical considerations, you can enhance your ability to positively influence outcomes across a spectrum of personal and professional situations. Ultimately, being likable isn't just about being agreeable—it's about fostering genuine connections that are mutually beneficial and fulfilling.

CHAPTER 6: THE LAW OF SCARCITY

The Value of the Rare

The Law of Scarcity captures a fundamental economic and psychological principle: items that are scarce, or perceived as scarce, are often valued more highly than those that are readily available. This principle taps into the human tendency to prioritize things that are in limited supply, driven by the fear of missing out (FOMO) and the desire to possess what is exclusive.

Psychological Roots of Scarcity

The allure of scarcity is deeply embedded in our psychology. It is linked to several behavioral tendencies:

1. **Loss Aversion**: Humans are generally more motivated by the fear of losing something than by the prospect of gaining something of equivalent value. Scarcity amplifies this effect by heightening the stakes of potential loss.

2. **Competition**: Scarcity naturally induces a sense of competition. We often want what others want, especially when it is in limited supply, as obtaining it not only satisfies a desire but also signifies a win against competitors.

3. **Value Perception**: Scarce items are perceived as more valuable, often because their rarity is associated with greater quality, prestige, or uniqueness.

Scarcity in Marketing and Sales

Marketers and businesses often leverage scarcity to increase demand for products and services:

- **Limited-Time Offers**: Sales that are available for a limited period create a sense of urgency that encourages consumers to act quickly.

- **Exclusive Releases**: Products that are available in limited quantities or for a restricted audience can become highly coveted, often leading to a rush to purchase and even secondary markets where these items are sold at premium prices.

- **Seasonal Items**: Products that are only available at certain times of the year can draw significant attention and demand during their limited availability windows.

Strategies to Apply the Law of Scarcity

To effectively utilize the Law of Scarcity, consider the following approaches:

1. **Clearly Communicate Limits**: Make it clear when an offer or resource is limited. This could be through explicit statements about stock levels, time restrictions, or availability to specific groups.

2. **Highlight Competition**: Sometimes, simply knowing that others are also interested in an item can enhance its perceived value. Showing that others are buying or interested in a product can stimulate more interest.

3. **Create Exclusivity**: Develop exclusive products or memberships that offer unique benefits. This not only utilizes scarcity but can also foster a sense of belonging to an elite group.

Ethical Considerations

While scarcity is a powerful motivator, it must be employed ethically. Creating artificial scarcity to manipulate customers can lead to dissatisfaction and damage trust. Moreover, it's important to consider the implications of inciting panic buying or hoarding, especially for essential goods.

Cultural Contexts

Different cultures may react to scarcity in varied ways. For instance, in some cultures, the rush to acquire scarce items may be more pronounced due to higher collectivist values that emphasize group trends and actions. Understanding these nuances can help in tailoring approaches that are culturally sensitive and effective.

Conclusion

The Law of Scarcity is a dynamic tool in the arsenal of persuasion and influence. By understanding how scarcity affects perception and behavior, you can more effectively craft strategies that enhance the value and desirability of what you offer. Whether in marketing, product development, or personal interactions, recognizing and responsibly harnessing the power of scarcity can lead to significant advantages and successes.

CHAPTER 7: THE LAW OF CONSISTENCY

Harnessing the Drive for Consistency

The Law of Consistency is based on the principle that people have an inherent desire to be consistent with what they have previously said or done. This drive is not just a preference but a deep-seated need that affects our self-image and how others perceive us. When our actions are consistent with our beliefs and prior commitments, we experience a sense of self-satisfaction and are perceived by others as stable and trustworthy.

Psychological Underpinnings of Consistency

The need for consistency is rooted in the psychological desire to maintain a self-concept that is coherent and stable. Cognitive dissonance theory explains that when there is an inconsistency between our beliefs and our actions, it creates psychological discomfort, leading us to change one or the other to restore harmony. This drive can be a powerful lever in influencing behavior.

Consistency in Action

1. **Commitments and Beliefs**: Once people commit to something, especially publicly, they are more likely to follow through with actions that reinforce that commitment. This is because reneging on a commitment can cause internal dissonance and damage one's reputation.

2. **Behavioral Alignment**: People prefer to make choices that align with their previous actions and decisions. If you can frame requests or opportunities as extensions of past

behaviors, compliance becomes more likely.

Strategies for Leveraging Consistency

To effectively use the Law of Consistency, consider the following approaches:

1. **Small Initial Commitments**: Getting someone to agree to a small initial act that is in line with a larger behavior you desire can lead to greater compliance with the larger request later. This is known as the 'foot-in-the-door' technique.

2. **Public Declarations**: Encourage individuals to make their commitments public. Public commitments are more powerful because they involve social pressure and expectations, which further motivate individuals to stick to their words.

3. **Consistent Reminders**: Regularly reminding people of their past behaviors and commitments can reinforce their current and future actions in line with those behaviors.

Applications of the Law of Consistency

- **Marketing and Sales**: Marketers can encourage potential customers to make small, initial engagements, such as signing up for a newsletter or a free trial, which can later lead to more significant commitments like purchases.

- **Workplace Management**: In organizations, aligning new policies with the company's stated values and past practices can increase employee acceptance and adherence.

- **Social Influence**: In social movements or community-based initiatives, reminding participants of their previous support or actions can increase ongoing engagement and support.

Ethical Considerations

While the Law of Consistency is effective, it's crucial to use it ethically. Manipulating people into making commitments that they are uncomfortable with or that are against their best interests can lead to negative outcomes and damage relationships.

Cultural Variations

Cultural factors can influence how the Law of Consistency is perceived and acted upon. In cultures where social harmony and group cohesion are valued over individual expression, public commitments and the drive for consistent behavior might be even more influential.

Conclusion

The Law of Consanity is a nuanced tool that, when used responsibly, can significantly enhance the effectiveness of persuasive efforts. By understanding and respecting the natural human inclination for consistency, you can craft strategies that not only foster compliance but also build trust and credibility. This approach not only helps in achieving immediate goals but also in establishing long-term, reliable relationships.

CHAPTER 8: THE LAW
OF CONTRAST

The Power of Comparison

The Law of Contrast is based on the cognitive principle that our perceptions are not absolute but are influenced by the context in which they occur. When options are presented together, their differences are magnified in our minds, making one option appear significantly more appealing compared to the other. This psychological effect can be strategically employed to guide choices and influence decision-making processes.

Understanding Contrast

Contrast affects perception by enhancing the differences between comparative items. This can be observed in everyday life, such as when a moderately priced item is placed next to a high-priced item, making the former seem like a great deal in comparison. This effect leverages the human tendency to evaluate options relative to one another rather than in isolation.

Mechanisms of Contrast

1. **Relative Pricing**: By presenting a more expensive option first, subsequent options appear cheaper. This is often used in marketing strategies, where a premium product is shown alongside standard products to make the latter seem more affordable.

2. **Quality Perception**: Quality can also be contrasted effectively. When a high-quality item is showcased next to a lower-quality one, the superior features of the better item are highlighted, enhancing its desirability.

3. **Feature Highlighting**: Emphasizing the unique features of a product or service in comparison to another can accentuate its benefits, making it the preferred choice.

Strategies for Applying the Law of Contrast

To harness the power of contrast effectively, consider the following approaches:

1. **Anchoring with Premiums**: Start with the most expensive or high-end option as an anchor. This sets the tone for the perception of value and quality, against which all other options are judged.

2. **Decoy Options**: Introduce a third option that is less appealing but similar to one of the main choices. This decoy will make one of the other options look more attractive. This is commonly used in subscription models where the middle option is priced to make the highest option seem more valuable.

3. **Simplified Choices**: Reduce complexity by contrasting fewer options. Too many choices can lead to decision fatigue. Presenting fewer, clearly contrasted choices can guide decisions more effectively.

Applications in Various Fields

- **Sales**: Sales professionals can use contrast to make their products or services stand out by comparing features with those of competitors in a way that highlights their own advantages.

- **Negotiations**: In negotiations, starting with more extreme demands can make the final agreement appear more reasonable by contrast.

- **Advertising**: Advertisers often use contrasting before-and-after images to visually depict the effectiveness of a product, enhancing its perceived value.

Ethical Considerations

While effective, the use of contrast must be approached with ethical considerations. Misleading comparisons or manipulative pricing strategies can lead to consumer distrust and harm a brand's reputation. It is crucial to use contrast in a way that is honest and transparent.

Cultural Considerations

Cultural contexts can influence how contrast is perceived. In cultures with a high tolerance for ambiguity, subtle contrasts might be more effective, whereas in cultures that prefer clarity and certainty, more stark contrasts might be necessary.

Conclusion

The Law of Contrast is a powerful tool in the toolkit of persuasion. By understanding how to effectively present options in contrast, you can influence perceptions and steer decisions in a desired direction. Whether in marketing, sales, or everyday decision-making, applying this law thoughtfully can lead to more favorable outcomes and enhanced persuasive effectiveness.

CHAPTER 9: THE LAW OF REASONING

Harnessing the Power of Logic

The Law of Reasoning emphasizes the use of logical, reasoned arguments as a cornerstone of persuasion. In a world often swayed by emotional appeals, the ability to present clear, cogent, and rational arguments remains a powerful method to influence decisions and change minds. This chapter explores how logical reasoning can underpin persuasive efforts, providing a foundation that reinforces the emotional and psychological strategies discussed in previous chapters.

Understanding Logical Persuasion

Logical persuasion relies on the construction of arguments that are coherent, well-structured, and based on evidence. It appeals to the rational part of the human mind, encouraging individuals to reach conclusions through analysis and critical thinking. The effectiveness of logical arguments is rooted in their ability to make sense of complex issues, offering clarity and insight that can sway opinions and encourage action.

Components of Effective Reasoning

1. **Clarity of Argument**: Your argument should be clear and easily understandable. Avoid jargon and overly complex explanations that might obscure your main points.

2. **Relevance of Information**: Ensure that all information and examples you use directly support your argument. Irrelevant data can distract and weaken your case.

3. **Soundness of Logic**: Your conclusions should logically follow from your premises. Avoid logical fallacies, as these can

undermine the integrity of your argument and reduce your credibility.

Strategies for Applying Logical Persuasion

To effectively employ the Law of Reasoning, consider these strategies:

1. **Structure Your Arguments**: Use a recognizable structure such as the classic "problem-solution-benefit" format. Start by identifying a problem, propose a solution, and outline the benefits of that solution.

2. **Use Evidence Effectively**: Support your arguments with appropriate evidence. This could include data, statistics, case studies, or authoritative quotes. Evidence increases the perceived validity of your arguments.

3. **Anticipate Objections**: Prepare for potential counterarguments by addressing them within your presentation. This not only shows thorough preparation but also positions you as fair and balanced.

4. **Simplify Complex Ideas**: Break down complex ideas into simpler, digestible parts. Use analogies, metaphors, or diagrams to make abstract concepts more concrete and relatable.

Applications in Various Contexts

- **Business Negotiations**: In negotiations, the ability to present logical arguments can help clarify the stakes and benefits, leading to more fruitful outcomes.

- **Educational Settings**: Teachers and educators often rely on logical reasoning to explain new concepts and persuade students of the validity of certain theories or methods.

- **Public Speaking and Debates**: Effective public speakers use structured reasoning to build compelling arguments that resonate with their audiences.

Ethical Considerations

While reasoning is a powerful tool, it must be used ethically. Manipulating facts or misrepresenting information to make an argument appear stronger is unethical and can damage trust and credibility.

Cultural Variations

Different cultures place varying levels of emphasis on logical reasoning. In some cultures, emotional and relational aspects might be more persuasive, while in others, a strong logical argument is highly valued. Understanding these cultural nuances is key to effectively using reasoning in international or diverse contexts.

Conclusion

The Law of Reasoning provides a robust framework for enhancing your persuasive efforts through logical arguments. By crafting clear, relevant, and well-supported arguments, you can engage the rational minds of your audience, leading to more informed, thoughtful decisions. This approach not only strengthens your persuasive capacity but also contributes to a more rational and discerning society.

CHAPTER 10: THE LAW OF EMOTIONAL APPEAL

The Role of Emotions in Decision-Making

While logic plays a critical role in persuasion, emotions are equally, if not more, influential in shaping decisions. The Law of Emotional Appeal recognizes that most decisions, even those that appear rational, are profoundly influenced by emotional factors. Emotions can bypass cognitive processing to trigger fast, automatic reactions, which is why appealing to them can dramatically enhance the effectiveness of persuasive efforts.

Understanding Emotional Influence

Emotions serve as a shortcut in decision-making, allowing individuals to quickly assess situations based on how they feel rather than extensive deliberation. This process is not just a matter of convenience but a necessary function in a world where rapid responses can be crucial. Emotions also help encode memories, making emotionally charged experiences more memorable than those that are not.

Components of Emotional Persuasion

1. **Identify Key Emotions**: Understanding the specific emotions that drive your audience is crucial. Fear, joy, sadness, and pride can all be leveraged differently to motivate action.

2. **Emotional Contagion**: Emotions are contagious. Expressing genuine emotions can cause others to feel the same way, due to the mirror neuron system in the human brain.

3. **Storytelling**: Narratives are powerful tools for emotional engagement. Stories allow individuals to experience emotions vicariously and can make complex issues more relatable and impactful.

Strategies for Applying the Law of Emotional Appeal

To effectively harness emotional influence, consider the following approaches:

1. **Use Emotional Triggers**: Craft messages that trigger emotional responses relevant to the action you want people to take. For example, charities often use images of those in need to elicit empathy and compassion, which can increase donations.

2. **Appeal to Values and Beliefs**: Connect your message to what your audience cares about deeply. Aligning your message with their values can evoke strong emotional responses and drive commitment.

3. **Create Experiential Moments**: Design experiences that elicit strong emotional reactions. This could be through immersive events, interactive content, or personal stories that make the emotional experience vivid and real.

4. **Utilize Visuals and Music**: Visual and auditory elements can enhance emotional impact. Thoughtfully chosen images, colors, and music can amplify the emotional tone of your message.

Applications Across Fields

- **Marketing and Advertising**: Brands frequently use emotional appeals to create strong connections with their audience, making their messages more memorable and impactful.

- ` **Political Campaigning**: Politicians use emotional appeals to energize their base, garner support, and drive voter turnout.

- **Public Health Campaigns**: Emotional appeals are often used to change health behaviors, such as campaigns to stop smoking or encourage healthy eating.

Ethical Considerations

While emotional appeals are powerful, they must be used responsibly. Manipulating emotions can lead to unethical outcomes, such as fearmongering or misinformation. It's important to use emotional appeals to inform and enhance understanding rather than to deceive or coerce.

Cultural Sensitivity

The effectiveness of emotional appeals can vary significantly across different cultures, which may have different emotional expressions and triggers. Understanding and respecting these differences is crucial when crafting messages intended for diverse audiences.

Conclusion

The Law of Emotional Appeal is a vital component of effective persuasion. By understanding and strategically engaging the emotions of your audience, you can greatly enhance the impact of your messages. Whether in marketing, leadership, or personal interactions, effectively leveraging emotions can lead to deeper connections and more profound influences on decision-making.

4

Chapter 11: The Law of Expectation - Explore how people often conform to the expectations set for them, and how this can be strategically used in influencing others.

ChatGPT

Chapter 11: The Law of Expectation

Harnessing Expectations for Influence

The Law of Expectation revolves around the powerful notion that individuals often rise or fall to meet the expectations set for them. This psychological principle can significantly shape behaviors and outcomes, making it a crucial tool for effective influence and leadership. Expectations, whether communicated explicitly or implicitly, serve as a guiding force, subtly directing how people think, perform, and interact.

Psychological Basis of Expectations

Expectations work by setting a predefined standard that individuals naturally strive to meet. This phenomenon is partly explained by the self-fulfilling prophecy, where believing something can make it come true, primarily because the belief influences behavior towards making it a reality. People internalize the expectations set for them and often adjust their actions to align with these anticipations.

Key Components of Expectation Influence

1. **Positive vs. Negative Expectations**: Positive expectations tend to elevate performance by boosting confidence and motivation. Conversely, negative expectations can lead to a decrease in effort and self-esteem, often fulfilling the prophecy of failure.

2. **Clarity and Communication**: Clearly articulated expectations are more likely to be met. It's important for leaders, educators, or influencers to communicate expectations effectively and transparently.

3. **Credibility**: The source of the expectation affects its power. Expectations from a respected and credible source are more likely to be taken seriously and strived for.

Strategies for Applying the Law of Expectation

To effectively leverage the Law of Expectation, consider the following approaches:

1. **Set High, but Achievable, Expectations**: Establishing high expectations can lead to higher performance, provided the goals are seen as attainable. This encourages people to stretch their capabilities without feeling overwhelmed.

2. **Communicate Expectations Consistently**: Reinforce expectations through regular communication and feedback.

This not only reminds individuals of the standards expected of them but also provides them with a sense of direction and purpose.

3. **Align Expectations with Individual Goals**: People are more likely to meet expectations that resonate with their personal ambitions and values. Aligning your expectations with the individual's goals can enhance motivation and engagement.

4. **Model the Expected Behavior**: Demonstrating the behavior you expect from others can be a powerful motivator. Leaders who "walk the talk" are more likely to inspire their teams to meet the expectations set.

Applications Across Various Contexts

- **Education**: Teachers who expect high performance from their students often see better outcomes, as students strive to meet these expectations.

- **Management**: Managers can use expectation settings to improve team performance, ensuring that each member knows what is expected and feels supported to achieve these goals.

- **Personal Relationships**: Setting mutual expectations in personal relationships can improve communication and reduce conflicts, as both parties have a clear understanding of what to expect from each other.

Ethical Considerations

While powerful, the manipulation of expectations must be approached ethically. Unrealistic or unfair expectations can lead to stress, burnout, and disillusionment. It's crucial to consider the well-being of those from whom you are setting expectations.

Cultural Considerations

Cultural norms can influence how expectations are set and met. For instance, in high-context cultures, expectations may be communicated more indirectly, requiring sensitivity and awareness to decode and understand them correctly.

Conclusion

The Law of Expectation is a subtle yet potent tool in the arsenal of influence. By understanding and strategically managing expectations, you can significantly impact the attitudes, behaviors, and performances of others. This law not only fosters higher levels of achievement but also builds a framework for accountability and growth within any organizational or personal context.

CHAPTER 12: THE LAW OF CONTEXT

The Influence of Environment on Behavior

The Law of Context posits that the environment and situational factors surrounding individuals significantly influence their behaviors and decisions. Context shapes perception, mood, and action, often in subtle but profound ways. Understanding how these elements operate allows for more effective persuasion and influence, by aligning messages and actions with the environmental cues that people unconsciously respond to.

Exploring the Role of Context

Context includes everything from physical surroundings to social settings, cultural backgrounds, and temporal conditions. It forms the backdrop against which decisions are made, acting as a lens through which situations are interpreted. This law is grounded in the psychological concept of situational attribution, where individuals assess their environment to determine appropriate responses.

Key Aspects of Contextual Influence

1. **Physical Environment**: The design, layout, and ambience of a space can dramatically affect how individuals feel and behave. For example, retail environments use lighting, music, and layout to influence consumer behavior and decision-making.

2. **Social Context**: The presence and behavior of others can heavily influence an individual's actions. Social norms and

peer pressures play critical roles, guiding behavior in both conscious and unconscious ways.

3. **Cultural Background**: Cultural contexts affect how messages are perceived and interpreted. What works in one cultural setting may not work in another, due to differing values, norms, and expectations.

4. **Temporal Factors**: The timing of an event or decision can influence outcomes. Factors like time of day, deadlines, and historical timing (such as economic or political climate) can all impact decision-making.

Strategies for Leveraging the Law of Context

To effectively apply the Law of Context, consider the following strategies:

1. **Adapt to Physical Settings**: Tailor your approach to fit the physical environment. For instance, in a busy, noisy setting, use clear and concise messaging; in a calm, intimate setting, a more detailed, narrative approach might be more effective.

2. **Utilize Social Proof**: Harness the power of the social context by demonstrating popular support or approval for your initiatives. People are more likely to engage in behaviors that they see others doing, especially peers or role models.

3. **Respect Cultural Norms**: Always consider the cultural dimensions of your audience. Adapt your messages to align with local customs and expectations to enhance receptivity and effectiveness.

4. **Optimize Timing**: Choose the right moment to introduce ideas or make requests. Timing your actions around when people are most receptive—such as after positive news or during a period of stability—can increase their impact.

Applications Across Fields

- **Marketing and Sales**: Marketers can enhance campaigns by aligning them with the context in which the advertisements will be seen, considering both the physical and social environments of their target audience.

- **Policy and Public Health**: Public health campaigns can be more effective when they account for the cultural and social contexts of the communities they aim to influence, tailoring messages to fit local norms and values.

- **Workplace Efficiency**: Employers can boost productivity and morale by designing workspaces that consider human factors like light, space, and ergonomics, and by fostering a cultural environment that promotes well-being.

Ethical Considerations

While context can be a powerful tool for influence, it's important to use this knowledge ethically. Manipulating environments in ways that coerce or deceive individuals into making decisions against their will or best interest can lead to harm and erode trust.

Conclusion

The Law of Context underscores the importance of considering the surrounding environment when attempting to influence behavior and make decisions. By understanding and strategically adjusting to these contextual factors, influencers can significantly enhance the effectiveness of their efforts, leading to more successful and harmonious outcomes.

CHAPTER 13: THE LAW OF PAIN AND PLEASURE

Understanding the Motivational Forces of Pain and Pleasure

The Law of Pain and Pleasure posits that the two most fundamental drivers of human behavior are the avoidance of pain and the pursuit of pleasure. These primal instincts govern much of our decision-making, pushing us towards actions that enhance our well-being and away from those that threaten it. By recognizing and strategically applying these motivators, influencers can craft messages that resonate deeply, prompting desired behaviors and responses.

Psychological Basis of Pain and Pleasure

Pain and pleasure are not merely physical sensations but are deeply embedded psychological states that influence cognitive processes and emotional responses. The brain is hardwired to prioritize these sensations because they signal either threats or rewards:

1. **Pain Avoidance**: Often considered a stronger motivator than the pursuit of pleasure, pain avoidance is rooted in survival instincts. The anticipation of discomfort or loss can provoke immediate and powerful responses.

2. **Pleasure Seeking**: The pursuit of pleasure is associated with reward pathways in the brain. Activities that induce pleasure reinforce behaviors and create patterns likely to be repeated.

Leveraging Pain and Pleasure in Persuasion

Effective persuasive messaging often involves framing choices in terms of pain and pleasure. Here's how this can be implemented:

1. **Highlight Benefits (Pleasure)**: Emphasize the positive outcomes and benefits of a decision or behavior. Show how taking action will lead to pleasure, satisfaction, or gain. For instance, marketing campaigns often highlight the enjoyment or status derived from owning a product.

2. **Emphasize Consequences (Pain)**: Detail what might be lost by not taking action. This could involve outlining the negatives of maintaining the status quo or the potential downsides of missing an opportunity. For example, public health campaigns might focus on the severe health risks of smoking to encourage cessation.

3. **Balance Appeals**: While pain might be a stronger immediate motivator, solely relying on it can cause anxiety or backlash. Balancing the negative with the promise of positive rewards can create a more compelling, holistic appeal.

Applications Across Various Contexts

- **Marketing and Advertising**: Advertisers might create campaigns that either focus on the joy of using a product or the fear of missing out if one doesn't purchase it.

- **Behavior Change Programs**: Programs aimed at changing behaviors, such as fitness regimens or educational courses, can use these principles by emphasizing the personal growth and success that come from completing the program, while also discussing the consequences of inaction.

- **Therapeutic Contexts**: In therapy, understanding a client's pain points and desired pleasures can help in crafting strategies for coping and improvement.

Ethical Considerations

While powerful, using pain and pleasure in persuasion must be handled with ethical care. Manipulating these emotions can lead to undue stress or unrealistic expectations. Ethical persuasion respects the autonomy of the audience and provides a balanced view that helps individuals make informed decisions based on both the benefits and the risks.

Conclusion

The Law of Pain and Pleasure is a foundational element in understanding human behavior and can be a potent tool in the art of persuasion. By appealing to these intrinsic motivators, influencers can craft messages that not only move people to action but also resonate on a deep emotional level. However, the responsible use of this law involves providing true and balanced information that empowers rather than manipulates the audience.

CHAPTER 14: THE LAW OF STORIES

Harnessing the Power of Storytelling

The Law of Stories underscores the profound impact that well-crafted narratives have on human cognition and emotion. Stories are more than just entertainment; they are a fundamental way through which humans process information and experience the world. Effective storytelling can make ideas stick, drive people to action, and forge connections that are both deep and lasting.

The Psychological Impact of Storytelling

Stories engage us in ways that facts and data alone cannot. They activate not just the language-processing parts of our brains but also the regions involved in experiencing emotions and envisioning actions. Here's why stories have such power:

1. **Emotional Engagement**: Stories naturally generate emotional responses. They can make us feel joy, sadness, anger, or excitement, emotions that are linked to memory and decision-making.

2. **Relatability**: Through characters and plots, stories allow audiences to see reflections of their own lives, which increases empathy and understanding.

3. **Memory Enhancement**: Narratives are easier to remember than abstract data. The structure of a story—its beginning, middle, and end—creates a "memory palace," where information is more easily recalled.

Elements of Effective Storytelling

To leverage storytelling in persuasion, it's crucial to understand the elements that make stories compelling:

1. **Characters**: Characters are the heart of any story. They should be relatable and flawed, allowing the audience to see parts of themselves in the characters' struggles and triumphs.

2. **Conflict**: Conflict is what drives a story forward. It introduces tension and keeps the audience engaged, eager to find out how the conflict will be resolved.

3. **Resolution**: A satisfying resolution provides closure, offers a lesson, or calls to action. It's where the moral or message of the story is crystallized.

Strategies for Incorporating Stories in Persuasive Messaging

1. **Use Personal Stories**: Personal stories or anecdotes are highly effective because they seem authentic and build trust. Sharing your own experiences related to the topic can make your message more credible and engaging.

2. **Incorporate Metaphors and Analogies**: These can help explain complex ideas in a simple and imaginative way, making your message more accessible and memorable.

3. **Create Scenarios**: Imagine scenarios that vividly illustrate the consequences of decisions. For example, in a campaign about safety, describe a scenario where a simple safety measure could prevent a disastrous outcome.

4. **Employ Visual Storytelling**: Combine narratives with visuals. This can be especially powerful in video or multimedia presentations, where images and sound complement the verbal story.

Applications Across Various Fields

- **Marketing and Branding**: Brands use storytelling to create an emotional connection with customers, turning basic messages about products into compelling brand narratives.

- **Education**: Educators use stories to teach complex concepts, making them more tangible and understandable for students.

- **Leadership and Management**: Leaders use stories to inspire teams, communicate vision, and instill values that foster a strong organizational culture.

Ethical Considerations

The power of stories also comes with the responsibility to use them ethically. Stories should not manipulate or distort the truth. Instead, they should enhance understanding and encourage thoughtful decision-making.

Conclusion

The Law of Stories is a critical tool in the influencer's toolkit, capable of transforming abstract concepts into experiences that resonate on a deeply personal level. By mastering the art of storytelling, you can significantly enhance the impact and memorability of your messages, forging connections that motivate and endure.

CHAPTER 15: THE LAW OF REWARDS

Incentivizing Actions and Behaviors

T he Law of Rewards focuses on the power of incentives to motivate and shape behavior. By offering rewards, you can significantly influence individuals' actions, steering them towards desired outcomes. Rewards tap into both intrinsic and extrinsic motivations, making them a versatile tool for driving engagement and commitment.

Understanding the Mechanics of Rewards

Rewards function as positive reinforcements in behavior psychology, where the presence of a rewarding stimulus enhances the likelihood of repeating the associated behavior. This principle is rooted in the operant conditioning theory, which posits that behaviors followed by favorable consequences are likely to recur.

Types of Rewards

1. **Extrinsic Rewards**: These are tangible rewards given from an external source, such as money, gifts, or other physical incentives. They are effective for motivating short-term actions and can be easily quantified and structured.

2. **Intrinsic Rewards**: These rewards are derived from the activity itself and are internally gratifying. They include feelings of accomplishment, personal growth, and fulfillment. Intrinsic rewards are crucial for long-term motivation and engagement.

Strategies for Implementing Effective Reward Systems

To maximize the effectiveness of rewards, consider the following approaches:

1. **Tailor Rewards to Individual Needs**: Different people are motivated by different types of rewards. Understanding your audience allows you to customize rewards that are most meaningful to them.

2. **Ensure Timeliness and Relevance**: Rewards should be given as soon as possible after the desired behavior to reinforce the connection between the action and the reward. They should also be relevant to the task or behavior being incentivized.

3. **Balance Extrinsic and Intrinsic Rewards**: While extrinsic rewards can provide immediate motivation, fostering intrinsic rewards can sustain long-term engagement and satisfaction. For example, offering professional development opportunities can motivate employees by aligning with their personal growth goals.

4. **Use Incremental Rewards**: Gradually increasing the reward as more is accomplished can encourage sustained effort and prevent complacency. This strategy keeps individuals motivated over longer periods.

Applications Across Various Fields

- **Corporate Settings**: Businesses often use reward systems to motivate employees, improve performance, and reduce turnover. Bonuses, raises, and promotions are common extrinsic rewards, while opportunities for career advancement provide intrinsic value.

- **Education**: Teachers use grades, certificates, and praise to motivate students, but they also build intrinsic motivation by making learning enjoyable and relevant.

- **Health and Wellness**: Fitness challenges often reward participants for reaching health goals, such as weight loss or steps walked, with prizes or social recognition.

Ethical Considerations

While rewards are powerful motivators, they must be used ethically. Over-reliance on extrinsic rewards can undermine intrinsic motivation, particularly if individuals become more focused on the rewards than the behaviors or goals themselves. It's important to ensure that rewards do not create unhealthy competition or unethical behaviors.

Conclusion

The Law of Rewards is an essential element of effective influence. By understanding and strategically applying various types of rewards, you can enhance motivation, guide behavior, and achieve desired outcomes. Whether in organizational settings, education, or personal development, a well-designed reward system can be a key to success, fostering both immediate results and long-term engagement.

CHAPTER 16: THE LAW OF REPUTATION

Cultivating a Powerful Asset

The Law of Reputation emphasizes the critical role of reputation in influencing interactions and shaping outcomes across all spheres of life. Reputation is not merely about being known; it's about being known for something specific. It can precede you in any room, setting the stage for how people will perceive and interact with you, and can be one of your most valuable assets or your biggest liability.

Foundation of Reputation

Reputation is built on a combination of trust, credibility, and past experiences others have had or heard about you. It involves the collective perception of your behavior and character over time and can significantly impact your ability to persuade and lead effectively.

Building a Strong Reputation

1. **Consistency**: Consistency in your actions, values, and communication is key to building a reliable reputation. People trust predictable patterns and consistency reassures them of your reliability and integrity.

2. **Expertise**: Establish yourself as an expert in your field. Continuously improve your skills and knowledge and share them through various platforms such as publications, speeches, and social media.

3. **Visibility**: To build a reputation, you need to be visible to the relevant audiences. Engage in community activities, professional organizations, and online platforms to increase

your visibility.

4. **Networking**: Building strong relationships within your industry and beyond can enhance your reputation. A robust network can act as ambassadors who spread positive word-of-mouth about you.

Maintaining Your Reputation

1. **Act with Integrity**: Always honor your commitments and be honest in all your dealings. Integrity is the cornerstone of a lasting reputation.

2. **Manage Online Presence**: In the digital age, much of your reputation is shaped online. Actively manage your social media profiles and be mindful of the content you post and share.

3. **Respond to Criticism Constructively**: How you handle criticism can significantly impact your reputation. Address issues transparently and strive to make amends if necessary. This shows maturity and respect for others.

4. **Continuous Improvement**: Stay aware of your weaknesses and work on them. Demonstrating a commitment to personal and professional growth can enhance your reputation over time.

Reputation in Negotiations and Interactions

In negotiations, a strong reputation can give you a significant advantage:

- **Trust and Leverage**: If you are known for being fair and effective, counterparts are more likely to enter negotiations with positive expectations and the willingness to compromise.

- **Precedent Setting**: A reputable figure sets a positive precedent in negotiations, as the opposing party is often more agreeable to terms, fearing the loss of future opportunities.

Ethical Considerations

The pursuit of a good reputation should not be driven by vanity or deception. It should be a reflection of genuine efforts to add value, maintain ethical standards, and contribute positively to the community.

Conclusion

The Law of Reputation underscores the importance of building and maintaining a reputation that not only precedes you but also enhances your ability to influence effectively. A well-managed reputation opens doors and builds bridges even before you step into a room, making it a pivotal element of successful personal and professional interactions.

CHAPTER 17: THE LAW OF MYSTERY

*Harnessing the Allure
of the Unknown*

The Law of Mystery revolves around the strategic use of uncertainty, secrecy, and intrigue to captivate attention and stimulate curiosity. Mystery provokes the human desire to resolve uncertainty, making it a powerful tool in maintaining interest and enhancing engagement. Whether in marketing, storytelling, or personal interactions, incorporating elements of mystery can make your messages and offers irresistibly compelling.

Psychological Appeal of Mystery

Mystery engages the brain's reward centers, specifically those activated by curiosity and the anticipation of new knowledge or experiences. This neurological response encourages continuous engagement as people seek to uncover the unknown and resolve the mystery.

1. **Curiosity Drive**: Mystery taps into the innate human drive for knowledge. When faced with incomplete information, people feel an irresistible urge to fill the gap, keeping them engaged with your message.

2. **Emotional Engagement**: Mystery often involves emotional elements such as suspense, surprise, and excitement, which can intensify the connection to the narrative or message.

3. **Perceived Value**: The less we know, the more we want to know. By withholding information, the perceived value of the revealed knowledge increases, making the final discovery

more satisfying and impactful.

Strategies for Incorporating Mystery

To effectively leverage the Law of Mystery, consider the following approaches:

1. **Tease Information Gradually**: Release information in pieces rather than all at once. This method keeps your audience coming back for more and builds anticipation for the next reveal.

2. **Create Cliffhangers**: Employ cliffhangers at strategic points in your narratives or presentations. This technique is especially effective in serialized content, where each segment ends with a suspenseful or unresolved moment that makes the audience eager for the next.

3. **Use Ambiguity**: Intentionally leave some elements open to interpretation. Ambiguity encourages discussion and speculation, which can increase engagement and interest in your message.

4. **Develop Enigmatic Characters or Brands**: Characters who have secrets or are surrounded by mystery often become the focus of attention. Similarly, brands that cultivate a mysterious or exclusive image can attract a loyal following eager to uncover what's hidden.

Applications of the Law of Mystery

- **Marketing and Advertising**: Products launched with teaser campaigns and enigmatic hints about their features can generate buzz and anticipation, leading to a successful market introduction.

- **Entertainment and Literature**: Movies, books, and games often rely on mystery to hook audiences, using complex plots and secretive characters to engage them deeply in the story.

- **Business and Innovation**: Companies can use mystery around upcoming innovations or business moves to keep competitors and the market intrigued and attentive.

Ethical Considerations

While mystery can be a potent tool, it must be used ethically. Creating false mysteries or using misleading tactics can lead to disappointment and distrust among your audience. Ensure that the resolution of the mystery is as rewarding and substantive as the build-up suggests.

Conclusion

The Law of Mystery is a nuanced tool in the art of persuasion and engagement. By wisely crafting messages and scenarios that include elements of mystery, you can captivate and maintain your audience's interest over extended periods. This approach not only enhances the allure of your messages or offers but also deepens the emotional and cognitive investment of your audience, leading to more profound and lasting impacts.

CHAPTER 18: THE LAW
OF ATTENTION

Mastering the Art of Captivation

The Law of Attention underscores the importance of not only capturing but also maintaining the attention of your audience. In an age saturated with information and distractions, securing the sustained focus of your audience is both a challenge and a critical factor for effective persuasion and influence.

Understanding the Dynamics of Attention

Attention is a limited resource. It is selective, can be divided, and is influenced by both internal states and external stimuli. Understanding how attention works can help you design your communications to break through the noise and engage your audience deeply.

Strategies for Capturing Attention

1. **Use of Strong Openings**: Begin with a statement, question, or visual that is surprising or emotionally engaging. The initial moments of your interaction set the tone and can hook your audience right from the start.

2. **Employ Visuals and Multimedia**: People are generally more attracted to and engaged by visual information. Using relevant and striking visuals can help draw and maintain attention.

3. **Incorporate Novelty**: Novelty causes the brain to pay attention because it's wired to notice new stimuli. Introducing new ideas, unusual facts, or creative presentations can spike interest and focus.

4. **Create Interactive Elements**: Interaction requires active participation, which naturally boosts attention. This can include live polls, Q&A sessions, or interactive demonstrations.

Strategies for Maintaining Attention

1. **Maintain a Dynamic Pace**: Vary the pace of your delivery and include changes in tone and volume. A dynamic presentation keeps the audience guessing and engaged.

2. **Use Storytelling**: As discussed in earlier chapters, stories not only capture but also maintain attention by building emotional connections with the audience. Weave narratives throughout your presentation to keep your audience engaged.

3. **Leverage the Power of Questions**: Asking questions, even rhetorical ones, can stimulate thinking and maintain engagement. Questions encourage your audience to consider their own views and anticipate answers.

4. **Segment Information**: Break down information into manageable and logically ordered segments. This helps maintain clarity and focus, preventing cognitive overload.

Applications Across Different Mediums

- **In Meetings and Presentations**: Utilize engaging openings, maintain eye contact, and use gestures to keep the audience's attention. Regularly prompt the audience with questions or reflections to keep them actively involved.

- **In Marketing and Advertising**: Brands can use bold imagery, catchy slogans, and interactive content to capture and hold consumer attention.

- **In Educational Settings**: Teachers and educators can use varied instructional methods, including multimedia, group discussions, and hands-on activities to engage students consistently.

Ethical Considerations

While capturing attention is crucial, it's important to do so ethically. Avoid using sensational or misleading content just to grab attention. The goal should be to engage your audience with integrity, providing value that justifies their focused attention.

Conclusion

The Law of Attention is essential for anyone looking to influence effectively in today's distracted world. By mastering the strategies to capture and maintain attention, you can ensure that your messages not only reach your audience but also resonate and motivate them.

CHAPTER 19: THE LAW OF ASSOCIATION

*Harnessing Connections for
Enhanced Influence*

The Law of Association underlines the power of linking ideas, concepts, or products with elements that are already positively perceived by your audience. This psychological tactic leverages the familiarity and favorability of known entities to enhance the attractiveness and credibility of new or less familiar ones. By skillfully associating your message or product with something your audience values or enjoys, you can significantly increase its appeal and persuasive potential.

Understanding the Power of Association

Associative learning is a fundamental human process, whereby an individual connects new information with existing knowledge or emotions. This connection often occurs subconsciously and can profoundly influence attitudes and decision-making. The Law of Association exploits this cognitive mechanism, making messages more memorable and impactful by linking them to well-regarded concepts or experiences.

Key Strategies for Utilizing Association

1. **Celebrity Endorsements**: One of the most visible forms of association is the use of celebrities in advertising. Celebrities transfer their appeal and the trust they command to the products they endorse, making these products more desirable to their fans.

2. **Brand Partnerships**: Collaborating with brands that have established a positive reputation can transfer some of that

positive sentiment to your own brand. This is especially effective when the brands share complementary values or target markets.

3. **Cultural Symbols**: Associating your message or product with well-liked cultural symbols (like national flags, famous landmarks, or traditional festivals) can evoke a strong emotional response, enhancing receptivity and attachment.

4. **Social Proof**: By showing that a product or idea is widely accepted or used by a group, especially a group admired or aspired to by the target audience, you can boost its acceptance and adoption. This is based on the principle that people feel more comfortable in following the lead of others they respect or relate to.

Effective Implementation of the Law of. Association

1. **Understand Your Audience**: Knowing what resonates with your audience is crucial. Tailor your associations to match their preferences, values, and cultural norms to ensure that the connections feel genuine and persuasive.

2. **Maintain Relevance**: The associations you create should be relevant to the message or product. Irrelevant or forced associations can confuse the audience or seem manipulative, undermining trust and effectiveness.

3. **Use Visuals**: Visual associations can be particularly powerful. Use images, colors, and designs that evoke the desired associations and reinforce the connection at a glance.

4. **Consistency**: Consistent use of associations across different channels and over time helps to reinforce the desired connections and deepen the impact. This consistency should be maintained in messaging, imagery, and overall branding.

Applications Across Various Fields

- **Marketing**: Marketers often use associative strategies to position new products in the market by linking them with popular events, lifestyles, or public figures.

- **Politics and Public Policy**: Politicians and advocates frequently associate their campaigns with popular values or historical figures to gain credibility and support.

- **Education and Public Health**: Educational and public health campaigns can be more effective when they link their messages to well-liked activities or widely respected figures within the community.

Ethical Considerations

While the Law of Association is a powerful tool, it must be used ethically. Avoid deceptive or manipulative associations that could mislead the public. Associations should be transparent and honest to maintain credibility and trust with your audience.

Conclusion

The Law of Association is a potent mechanism in the arsenal of persuasion. By strategically connecting your ideas or products with something already valued by your audience, you can enhance their attractiveness and persuasive power. This approach not only elevates the perceived value of what you are promoting but also builds a stronger, more emotional connection with your audience.

CHAPTER 20: THE LAW
OF BALANCE

Harmonizing Logic and Emotion

The Law of Balance emphasizes the strategic integration of both logical and emotional appeals in persuasion to effectively engage diverse audiences. This dual approach is crucial because people are influenced by both rational thought and emotional feelings, often simultaneously. By balancing these elements, you can create messages that resonate more deeply and are more likely to motivate action.

Understanding the Interplay of Emotion and Logic

Emotions can drive immediate and powerful reactions, tapping into underlying values, fears, and desires. Logical arguments, on the other hand, appeal to reason, providing justification and credibility to claims. People are not solely rational or emotional; they use both to make decisions. Thus, understanding when and how to appeal to each can enhance the effectiveness of communication.

Strategies for Balancing Emotional and Logical Appeals

1. **Know Your Audience**: Different audiences may require different balances of logic and emotion. For instance, technical professionals might prefer data-driven arguments, while creative professionals might respond better to narrative and emotional appeals.

2. **Start with Emotion, Follow with Logic**: Capture attention and create a connection using an emotional hook, then back up your message with logical arguments to provide depth and justification. This pattern leverages the initial

engagement and seals it with rational reasons.

3. **Use Stories to Bridge the Gap**: Stories can simultaneously evoke emotions and encapsulate logical arguments. They provide a scenario where listeners can emotionally invest while also receiving information that supports the narrative logically.

4. **Visual and Statistical Harmony**: Combine impactful visuals that evoke emotions with charts and statistics that appeal to the logical side. This combination can make complex information more accessible and memorable.

Effective Implementation of the Law of Balance

1. **Tailor Messages for Context**: The balance of emotional and logical appeals might shift based of the context and medium of communication. For example, social media might lean more towards emotional appeals due to its rapid, visual nature, whereas academic or professional presentations might require a stronger emphasis on logic and data.

2. **Feedback and Adjustment**: Use feedback from your audience to adjust the balance of logic and emotion. Paying attention to how people respond during and after your message can provide valuable insights into their preferences and the effectiveness of your approach.

3. **Ethical Considerations**: Ensure that your use of emotional appeals is ethical and does not manipulate or exploit your audience's fears or desires unjustly. Similarly, ensure that logical appeals are based on accurate and relevant information.

Applications Across Various Fields

- **Marketing and Advertising**: Marketers often balance emotional appeals (e.g., happiness associated with a product) with logical information (e.g., cost savings, product features) to persuade consumers effectively.

- **Public Speaking and Leadership**: Leaders and speakers may start presentations with personal anecdotes to connect emotionally, then pivot to detailed evidence and logical arguments to substantiate their points.

- **Healthcare and Public Policy**: Campaigns that aim to change behaviors or promote policies can use emotional narratives to highlight significance and statistical data to reinforce the message's validity and urgency.

Conclusion

The Law of Balance is a foundational principle for effective persuasion across all communication forms. By skillfully blending emotional and logical elements, you can craft messages that are both compelling and credible, maximizing your influence and achieving greater impact with your audience. This balanced approach not only caters to the complex nature of human decision-making but also builds trust and credibility through thoughtful communication.

CHAPTER 21: THE LAW OF FREQUENCY

Maximizing Impact Through Repetition

The Law of Frequency states that repeated exposure to a message increases its recognition, retention, and likelihood of being acted upon. This principle is grounded in the psychological concept of the "mere exposure effect," which suggests that people tend to develop a preference for things merely because they are familiar with them. By strategically repeating a message, you can enhance its effectiveness, making it more likely that your audience will remember and embrace it.

The Cognitive Basis of Repetition

Repetition works by strengthening the neural pathways associated with the specific information or message, making it easier for the brain to access and recall this information. Repetition also counters the natural tendency to forget, which is a challenge in today's information-saturated environment where attention is a scarce commodity.

Effective Strategies for Implementing the Law of Frequency

1. **Consistent Messaging**: Ensure that the core message remains consistent across all repetitions. Consistency helps in reinforcing the message and avoiding confusion among the audience.

2. **Vary the Delivery**: While the core message should remain consistent, vary the format and delivery to keep it engaging. This can involve changing the medium, the visuals, the

spokesperson, or even the style of presentation while keeping the underlying message the same.

3. **Space Out Repetitions**: Distribute the repetitions over time rather than clustering them closely together. Spaced repetition is a technique proven to improve memory and recall, as it allows time for the information to be consolidated in the brain.

4. **Integrate Across Platforms**: Utilize multiple platforms and media to repeat the message. This can include digital media, print, television, and face-to-face interactions, each reinforcing the same core message in different contexts.

Applications of the Law of Frequency

- **Advertising and Marketing**: Marketers use frequency to ensure brand messages and product information are internalized by consumers. Successful campaigns often feature a memorable tagline or jingle repeated across various media.

- **Educational Settings**: Educators repeat key concepts in different contexts and through various methods to help students internalize and remember important information.

- **Public Health Campaigns**: Repetition is crucial in public health messaging to ensure that important health behaviors are adopted by the community. Frequent reminders about health practices like handwashing or vaccinations can significantly improve compliance and outcomes.

- **Corporate Communication**: In corporate settings, reinforcing company values and strategic objectives frequently helps keep employees aligned and motivated towards common goals.

Ethical Considerations

While repetition is a powerful tool, it must be used ethically. Overuse can lead to annoyance and can be perceived as manipulation, potentially leading to disengagement and distrust among the audience. It is important to balance frequency with respect for the audience's attention and intelligence.

Conclusion

The Law of Frequency is essential for ensuring that messages are not only heard but remembered and acted upon. By carefully planning how and when a message is repeated, you can effectively increase its impact, ensuring that it resonates with the audience and drives the desired action. Whether in marketing, education, public health, or any other field, mastering the art of repetition can significantly enhance the effectiveness of your communication efforts.

CHAPTER 22: THE LAW OF INVESTMENT

Deepening Commitment
Through Personal Investment

T he Law of Investment states that the more effort and resources people invest into an idea, task, or object, the more they value and commit to it. This principle is rooted in cognitive and behavioral psychology, particularly around concepts like cognitive dissonance and effort justification. When individuals dedicate time, energy, or other resources, they naturally seek to justify their investment by enhancing their commitment and perception of the value of the outcome.

Understanding the Dynamics of Investment

Investment can take many forms, including financial contributions, time, emotional energy, and intellectual input. The key aspect of investment is that it involves personal contribution, which leads to a stronger connection and commitment to the outcome. Here's how investment influences behavior and perception:

1. **Effort Justification**: When people work hard for something, they tend to value it more highly than if it were given to them with little or no effort. This is because they need to justify the effort spent, often enhancing the perceived worth of the result.

2. **Increased Commitment**: Making an investment can lock individuals into a pathway, increasing their commitment to seeing a project or task through to completion. This

commitment often grows with continued investment.

3. **Cognitive Dissonance Reduction**: If individuals invest significantly in something that does not immediately meet their expectations, they are likely to adjust their perceptions to reduce dissonance between their expectations and reality.

Strategies for Leveraging the Law of Investment

To effectively utilize the Law of Investment in influencing behavior and decision-making, consider the following approaches:

1. **Encourage Initial Involvement**: Get your audience to invest early, even if the initial investment is minimal. This could be as simple as asking for opinions, getting them to sign up for a newsletter, or participating in a survey.

2. **Gradually Increase Levels of Investment**: Once the initial investment is made, encourage progressively greater investments. This method can be particularly effective in contexts like educational courses, membership programs, or long-term projects.

3. **Provide Ownership Opportunities**: When people feel a sense of ownership over a process or product, they are more likely to invest further and value it more. Customization features or participatory design processes can enhance this feeling of ownership.

4. **Recognize and Reward Investments**: Acknowledge the contributions and efforts of individuals. Recognition not only validates their investment but also motivates further involvement and loyalty.

Applications Across Various Fields

- **Marketing and Sales**: Businesses can create loyalty programs where customers earn rewards for their purchases, encouraging continued investment and increasing perceived value.

- **Workplace Productivity**: Employers can encourage

employees to invest in their own professional development by providing matching funds for training programs or offering time off for educational pursuits.

- **Non-profit and Advocacy**: Non-profits can engage supporters by encouraging volunteerism. The time and effort volunteers invest can lead to stronger commitment and higher lifetime value to the organization.

Ethical Considerations

While encouraging investment can lead to positive outcomes, it is important to ensure that it does not exploit or manipulate. Individuals should always be made aware of what they are committing to and the potential risks involved. Investments should be proportional to the rewards, and expectations should be managed transparently.

Conclusion

The Law of Investment is a powerful tool for deepening commitment and enhancing the perceived value of an endeavor. By understanding and strategically facilitating investment from your audience or stakeholders, you can build more enduring relationships, drive stronger commitments, and create more meaningful results. This approach not only benefits the immediate goals but also fosters long-term loyalty and engagement.

CHAPTER 23: THE LAW OF TIMING

Optimizing Moments for Influence

T he Law of Timing centers on the crucial role that timing plays in the effectiveness of persuasion. The impact of a message can vary significantly depending on when it is delivered. Timing can influence how a message is received, how much attention it gets, and how persuasive it is. Understanding and capitalizing on optimal timing can dramatically enhance the success of your communication efforts.

Understanding Timing in Persuasion

Timing in persuasion involves more than just choosing the right moment to act; it encompasses understanding the context, the emotional state of the audience, and the broader environment in which the message is delivered. It requires sensitivity to both macro-scale conditions (like economic or cultural climates) and micro-scale situations (such as individual readiness to receive a message).

Key Aspects of Effective Timing

1. **Readiness**: Deliver your message when the audience is most receptive. This could be determined by their emotional state, the completion of prerequisite steps, or their demonstrated interest in related topics.

2. **Cultural and Social Contexts**: Consider broader social or cultural events that might affect receptivity. For example, launching a new product or initiative around times of positive societal change can capitalize on a general feeling of optimism.

3. **Avoiding Conflicts**: Avoid delivering important messages when they might be overshadowed by competing events or when the audience might be distracted or stressed by other concerns.

4. **Seizing Opportunities**: Sometimes, unexpected opportunities arise that provide an ideal moment for persuasion. Being flexible and ready to seize these moments can make a significant difference.

Strategies for Leveraging the Law of Timing

To effectively leverage timing in your persuasive efforts, consider the following strategies:

1. **Monitor Trends and Patterns**: Keep an eye on trends, both in your specific field and in the broader cultural landscape. Anticipating shifts can help you time your messages to coincide with these trends.

2. **Use Timing to Create Urgency**: Setting deadlines or limited-time offers can create a sense of urgency, prompting quicker decision-making and commitment.

3. **Align with Audience Rhythms**: Understand the daily, weekly, or seasonal rhythms of your audience. Timing your message to fit into these rhythms can increase its impact, such as targeting business professionals on weekday mornings or young audiences in the evenings.

4. **Test and Learn**: Use analytics and feedback to test the effectiveness of different timing strategies. Learning what works best for your audience and adjusting your approach accordingly is key to mastering the Law of of Timing.

Applications Across Various Fields

- **Marketing**: For marketers, timing product launches, sales promotions, and advertising campaigns can affect the overall success of these initiatives.

- **Politics**: Politicians must time their campaigns and key messages to coincide with election cycles and public sentiment.

- **Management and Leadership**: Leaders must choose the right moments to initiate change or communicate important decisions to ensure alignment and buy-in from their teams.

Ethical Considerations

While strategic timing is valuable, it's important to consider its ethical implications. Timing should not be used to manipulate or coerce decisions from people who are vulnerable or in distress. Instead, it should be used to enhance the relevance and helpfulness of the information provided.

Conclusion

The Law of Timing is a potent aspect of persuasion that requires careful consideration and strategic planning. By understanding and respecting the nuances of timing, you can significantly enhance the effectiveness of your communications, making them more persuasive and impactful. Whether in marketing, leadership, or everyday interactions, effective timing can be the difference between a message that resonates and one that falls flat.

CHAPTER 24: THE LAW OF UNITY

Fostering Connection Through Shared Identity

T he Law of Unity is centered on the principle that a sense of belonging and shared identity significantly enhances the persuasive appeal of ideas, products, and movements. When people feel that they are part of a group or movement, their alignment with its goals and values intensifies, making them more receptive to messages and more willing to act in accordance with group norms.

Understanding the Role of Unity in Persuasion

Unity taps into deep-seated psychological needs for belonging and identity. Social identity theory explains how individuals derive part of their sense of self from the groups to which they belong. This alignment not only affects self-conception but also influences behavior, as people are driven to think and act in ways that are congruent with the perceived identity of the group.

Key Aspects of Unity

1. **Common Goals and Values**: Unity is strengthened by shared goals and values. When a group or movement clearly articulates what it stands for, members can align themselves more closely with its objectives.

2. **Inclusivity**: Creating a sense of inclusivity can enhance feelings of unity. This involves making sure that members feel valued and that their contributions are recognized.

3. **Symbolism**: Symbols, rituals, and traditions can reinforce a

sense of collective identity and belonging. These elements serve as constant reminders of the group's unity and purpose.

4. **Communication:** Regular and transparent communication helps maintain and strengthen the bonds of unity. It ensures that all members feel informed and involved in the group's activities.

Strategies for Leveraging the Law of Unity

To effectively employ the Law of Unity in your persuasive efforts, consider the following strategies:

1. **Emphasize Commonalities**: Highlight what your audience shares in common with each other and with your message or cause. This could be in terms of background, challenges, aspirations, or values.

2. **Create and Use Group Symbols**: Develop and use symbols, slogans, logos, or rituals that members can rally around. These symbols become markers of identity and tools of unity.

3. **Foster Interaction Among Members**: Facilitate opportunities for members to interact, share experiences, and collaborate on tasks. Interaction not only strengthens community bonds but also reinforces individual commitment to the group's goals.

4. **Narrative of Us vs. Them**: While it should be used cautiously and ethically, framing challenges or campaigns in terms of an "us vs. them" narrative can strengthen internal cohesion and clarify the group's purpose.

Applications Across Various Fields

- **Marketing and Branding**: Brands often create a sense of community among their customers, encouraging them to see themselves as part of a special group or lifestyle (e.g., Apple users).

- **Political Campaigns**: Politicians frequently appeal to unity by emphasizing shared heritage, values, or challenges, aiming to rally supporters around a common cause.

- **Organizational Management**: Leaders can enhance workplace motivation and cooperation by fostering a strong sense of organizational identity and collective purpose.

Ethical Considerations

The appeal to unity can be powerful but must be handled with ethical care. It should not be used to exclude, demonize, or unfairly disparage others who are outside the group. Furthermore, the sense of unity should not coerce individuals into conforming against their better judgment or individual ethical standards.

Conclusion

The Law of Unity is a profound force in persuasion, capable of deeply influencing both individual and group behaviors. By cultivating a sense of shared identity and belonging, you can significantly enhance the commitment of individuals to a cause or organization. Whether in marketing, social movements, or corporate settings, effectively harnessing the power of unity can lead to more cohesive, motivated, and effective groups.

CHAPTER 25: THE LAW OF SAFETY

Enhancing Appeal through Reassurance

The Law of Safety centers on the principle that people are naturally drawn to choices that make them feel secure and at ease. Providing a sense of safety and reassurance can significantly enhance the appeal of your messages and propositions, as it taps into the fundamental human need for security. When individuals feel safe, they are more likely to be receptive to new ideas, products, or changes.

Understanding the Importance of Safety in Decision-Making

Safety is a core human need, ranked highly on Maslow's hierarchy of needs, just after physiological requirements like food and shelter. This need for safety extends beyond physical well-being to include psychological and emotional security. In the context of persuasion, addressing this need can make your audience more open and trusting of your message.

Key Aspects of Providing Safety

1. **Risk Mitigation**: Demonstrating how your proposal reduces potential risks or prevents negative outcomes can make your message more compelling. This assurance can be particularly influential in high-stake decisions or investments.

2. **Transparency**: Openness in communication builds trust. By being transparent about intentions, processes, and the pros and cons of a proposition, you can alleviate fears and uncertainties.

3. **Consistency**: Regular and predictable actions foster a sense of reliability. Consistency in behavior, message delivery, and service reassures people that they can depend on what you say and offer.

4. **Social Proof**: Showcasing testimonials, endorsements, and widespread acceptance can provide social reassurance. Knowing that others have successfully engaged with an idea or product and benefited from it reduces the perceived risk.

Strategies for Leveraging the Law of Safety

To effectively employ the Law of Safety in your persuasive efforts, consider the following strategies:

1. **Highlight Protective Measures**: If your product or service involves potential risks, be upfront about these risks and emphasize the measures in place to mitigate them. This approach not only builds trust but also enhances the perceived value of your offering.

2. **Provide Guarantees and Warranties**: Offering guarantees or warranties can reduce the perceived risk associated with a purchase or commitment, making it safer for the customer to decide.

3. **Use Familiarity**: Introduce new ideas or changes in the context of familiar settings or by relating them to known concepts. This familiarity provides a safe frame of reference and can ease the acceptance process.

4. **Facilitate Easy Exits**: Letting people know they can opt out or reverse a decision can increase their willingness to engage. The option of an exit provides psychological reassurance and reduces perceived risk.

Applications Across Various Fields

- **Marketing and Sales**: Marketers can use safety appeals when promoting products that are designed to protect or enhance the user's security, such as insurance, health products, and security systems.

- **Organizational Change**: When introducing changes within an organization, leaders can focus on communicating how these changes will secure jobs, improve working conditions, or enhance career prospects.

- **Public Health**: In public health messaging, emphasizing safety can encourage compliance with recommendations meant to protect the community, such as vaccinations or preventive practices.

Ethical Considerations

While the appeal to safety is effective, it must be used responsibly. Fearmongering or exaggerating dangers to manipulate decisions undermines trust and can lead to long-term negative consequences.

Conclusion

The Law of Safety is a crucial aspect of persuasion, offering a pathway to influence by aligning with the intrinsic human desire for security. By thoughtfully incorporating elements of safety and reassurance into your messages, you can enhance their appeal, fostering a more trusting and receptive audience.

CHAPTER 26: THE LAW OF COMPARISON

Strategic Use of Comparative Analysis

The Law of Comparison highlights how people make decisions based on comparisons rather than absolute metrics. By understanding and strategically applying this principle, influencers can guide choices and significantly impact decision-making processes. People inherently evaluate their options by comparing them to others, whether consciously or unconsciously, and the framework you provide for these comparisons can heavily sway their conclusions.

Understanding Comparative Decision-Making

Comparative decision-making is rooted in cognitive psychology, particularly in how individuals assess value. The contrast effect, where the value of something is enhanced or diminished based on its comparison to something else, plays a crucial role. Setting the right comparative standards can make an option appear more favorable, less risky, or more beneficial.

Key Aspects of Effective Comparisons

1. **Anchoring**: The initial information people receive serves as an anchor for subsequent judgments. For example, presenting a high-priced item first can make the next option seem more affordable.

2. **Relativity**: People tend to evaluate options not on their standalone merits but relative to what is available. An item might not be appealing on its own but becomes attractive when compared to a lesser alternative.

3. **Context Framing**: The way options are presented—the context—can drastically influence perceptions. For instance, benefits highlighted in the context of loss prevention can seem more valuable than those framed merely as gains.

Strategies for Leveraging the Law of Comparison

To harness the Law of Comparison effectively, consider these approaches:

1. **Selective Comparisons**: Choose comparators that highlight the strengths of your proposition. By carefully selecting what you compare your product or idea against, you can predispose your audience to see it in a more favorable light.

2. **Control the Comparison Set**: Presenting a curated set of options can guide decisions more subtly. For example, adding a slightly higher-priced product with more features can make the originally intended product appear as a "smart buy."

3. **Decoy Effect**: Introduce an option designed to make another option look more appealing. Often, this decoy is not meant to be chosen but to make one of the other options stand out as a more rational choice.

4. **Simplify Choices**: Too many options can lead to decision fatigue. Simplifying choices by making the differences clear and straightforward can help guide the decision-making process more effectively.

Applications Across Various Fields

- **Marketing and Sales**: Marketers often use comparative pricing strategies or position new products relative to existing ones to influence consumer choice.

- **Negotiations**: In negotiations, presenting multiple proposal options can strategically steer the counterpart toward the preferred outcome by making it look more favorable in comparison.

- **Policy and Public Perception**: Policymakers can influence public opinion on new initiatives by comparing them with less effective or more costly alternatives, thereby highlighting their benefits.

Ethical Considerations

While comparisons can be a powerful tool for persuasion, they must be used ethically. Misleading comparisons, or those that distort the truth, can lead to short-term gains but long-term damage to credibility and trust.

Conclusion

The Law of Comparison is a fundamental principle in the psychology of decision-making. By understanding how comparisons shape perceptions and choices, influencers can craft more effective messages and strategies that lead to desired outcomes. Carefully managing the context and criteria of comparisons allows for a more controlled influence on decisions, ensuring that choices are both informed and beneficial.

CHAPTER 27: THE LAW OF ACKNOWLEDGMENT

Enhancing Influence
Through Transparency

The Law of Acknowledgment focuses on the strategic importance of recognizing and addressing doubts and objections upfront in any persuasive communication. By openly acknowledging potential reservations and concerns, you can build trust and credibility with your audience. This approach not only demonstrates confidence in your position but also respects the intelligence and concerns of your audience, making your arguments more persuasive and grounded.

Understanding the Dynamics of Acknowledgment

Acknowledging doubts and objections might seem counterintuitive, as it involves pointing out possible flaws or issues in your own arguments or proposals. However, this practice taps into the principles of honesty and transparency, which are critical for building lasting relationships and trust. Addressing objections head-on allows you to control the narrative and reinforce your arguments by preemptively resolving potential issues.

Key Benefits of Effective Acknowledgment

1. **Building Trust**: When you acknowledge potential negatives, your audience sees you as more honest and trustworthy. Trust is a crucial element in any relationship, particularly in contexts involving persuasion.

2. **Reducing Resistance**: Addressing objections before they are raised by the audience can preemptively reduce resistance.

When people see that their concerns are already considered and addressed, they are more likely to be receptive to the overall message.

3. **Enhancing Engagement**: Inviting and addressing questions encourages a more interactive and engaging communication process. It shows that you value the audience's input and are open to dialogue.

Strategies for Leveraging the Law of Acknowledgment

To apply the Law of Acknowledgment effectively, consider the following approaches:

1. **Research Common Concerns**: Understand and anticipate common objections or concerns related to your message or proposal. This preparation allows you to address these issues proactively in your communications.

2. **Incorporate Feedback Mechanisms**: Create opportunities for your audience to express doubts or concerns. This could be through Q&A sessions, surveys, or open forums. Actively listen to the feedback and integrate it into your response strategy.

3. **Use Testimonials and Case Studies**: Employ testimonials, case studies, or data that directly address potential objections. Showing real-life examples of how concerns were successfully managed can be highly persuasive.

4. **Frame Objections Positively**: When acknowledging objections, frame them in a way that highlights the strengths of your position. For example, "While it's true that implementing this software requires an initial investment, the efficiency gains and cost savings over time far outweigh the initial costs."

Applications Across Various Fields

• **Sales and Marketing**: Sales professionals can enhance their pitches by preemptively addressing potential customer objections, thereby smoothing the path to a sale.

- **Public Speaking and Debates**: Effective public speakers and debaters often acknowledge and refute counterarguments within their presentations to strengthen their own positions.

- **Customer Service and Support**: In customer service, acknowledging a customer's dissatisfaction and addressing it directly can lead to a more positive resolution and improve customer loyalty.

Ethical Considerations

While acknowledgment is a powerful tool, it must be used sincerely. Manipulative or insincere acknowledgment can backfire, leading to increased skepticism and decreased trust. Always ensure that your acknowledgments are genuine and that you truly address the concerns raised.

Conclusion

The Law of Acknowledgment is a pivotal strategy in enhancing the effectiveness of persuasive communication. By openly addressing doubts and objections, you not only build trust and reduce resistance but also demonstrate a depth of understanding and commitment to transparency. This approach fosters a more honest and constructive dialogue, crucial for achieving lasting influence and success.

4

Chapter 28: The Law of Curiosity - Discuss techniques for sparking and maintaining interest and curiosity, keeping people engaged.

ChatGPT

Chapter 28: The Law of Curiosity

Engaging Minds Through Exploration

The Law of Curiosity is based on the principle that human beings are naturally inclined to seek knowledge and understand their environment. By sparking and maintaining curiosity, you can keep people continuously engaged and motivated to learn more. Curiosity not only makes experiences enjoyable but also enhances the retention of information and encourages active participation.

Understanding Curiosity

Curiosity is driven by the desire to fill gaps in knowledge. When people encounter something that contradicts their existing understanding or presents a puzzle, their curiosity is piqued, prompting them to explore further to resolve their uncertainty. This process is both intellectually stimulating and emotionally rewarding, making it a powerful tool in education, marketing, and leadership.

Techniques for Sparking Curiosity

1. **Present Puzzles and Questions**: Start your communication with a thought-provoking question or an intriguing fact that challenges common assumptions. This method naturally leads the audience to want more information to resolve their curiosity.

2. **Tell Stories with Suspense**: Incorporate elements of mystery and suspense into your stories. Revealing information gradually can keep the audience on the edge of their seats, eager to learn what happens next.

3. **Create Information Gaps**: Introduce topics by highlighting what the audience will learn without giving away all the details upfront. This creates an information gap that people will be driven to close.

4. **Use Visuals and Interactive Content**: Engage sensory curiosity with striking visuals, interactive media, or hands-on demonstrations. These elements can make the learning process more engaging and memorable.

Strategies for Maintaining Curiosity

1. **Vary Content and Delivery**: Regularly introduce new topics, switch up your delivery methods, and use different media. Variety keeps the experience fresh and prevents boredom.

2. **Encourage Active Participation**: Involve your audience in

the learning or discovery process. Activities like group discussions, interactive tasks, or problem-solving exercises can enhance engagement and curiosity.

3. **Link to Wider Themes and Applications**: Show how specific information is connected to broader topics or real-world applications. This not only deepens understanding but also sparks curiosity about related subjects.

4. **Provide Pathways for Further Exploration**: At the end of a presentation or lesson, offer resources for further learning. This could be additional readings, websites, or follow-up projects that allow interested individuals to delve deeper.

Applications Across Various Fields

• **Education**: Educators can use curiosity-driven learning techniques to enhance student engagement and improve educational outcomes.

• **Marketing**: Marketers can create curiosity through teaser campaigns and mysterious ads that hint at new products or features, driving interest and anticipation.

• **Corporate Training**: Trainers can use curiosity to keep employees engaged in professional development. Introducing training sessions with a compelling question or challenge can increase participation and retention.

Ethical Considerations

While stimulating curiosity is generally positive, it must be done ethically. Avoid using "clickbait" tactics or providing misleading information just to pique interest. Such strategies can ultimately lead to distrust and disengagement.

Conclusion

The Law of Curiosity is a dynamic tool for capturing and sustaining attention and engagement. By understanding and applying the principles of curiosity in your communications and presentations, you can make them more engaging and effective. Curiosity not only enriches the experience but also deepens understanding and enhances learning, making it invaluable in any context where information needs to be conveyed effectively.

CHAPTER 29: THE LAW OF EXCLUSIVITY

Cultivating Desire through Rarity

The Law of Exclusivity underscores the compelling power of exclusivity in increasing the appeal and demand for a product, service, or experience. By offering exclusive access or products, you can create a sense of rarity and privilege that enhances perceived value and desirability. This strategy not only attracts interest but also builds a strong emotional connection, as people often value what they perceive as rare or hard to obtain.

Understanding Exclusivity

Exclusivity taps into several psychological mechanisms:

1. **Scarcity**: Similar to the scarcity principle, exclusivity implies limited availability, which can make offerings seem more valuable.

2. **Status**: Exclusive products or services often confer a sense of status or prestige on their owners, appealing to their desire for distinction and social recognition.

3. **Belonging**: While exclusivity by nature involves exclusion, for those included, it fosters a strong sense of belonging to an elite or select group.

Strategies for Leveraging Exclusivity

1. **Limited Editions**: Offering limited edition products can create a sense of urgency and exclusivity. Collectors and enthusiasts often place a higher value on items that are available only in limited quantities.

2. **Members-Only Access**: Creating members-only areas, services, or content can make membership more appealing. The exclusivity of access makes the membership itself a desirable commodity.

3. **Early Access**: Providing early access to products, services, or information to a select group of customers can increase loyalty and perceived value. Those granted early access feel valued and special, enhancing their connection to the brand.

4. **Personalization and Customization**: Offering personalized or customizable options can also create a form of exclusivity. When a product is tailored to an individual's preferences, it not only increases the item's value but also reduces the likelihood of an identical product being owned by someone else.

Applications Across Various Fields

- **Retail and Fashion**: High-end brands often release products in limited quantities to maintain high demand and luxury status. This approach is prevalent in the fashion industry, where exclusivity is synonymous with prestige.

- **Technology and Entertainment**: Tech companies might offer beta versions of new software to a select group of users, creating buzz and anticipation. In entertainment, early or exclusive releases can attract premium subscribers.

- **Service Industry**: Exclusive offers, such as VIP customer treatment or loyalty rewards, can enhance consumer loyalty and increase perceived service value.

Ethical Considerations

While exclusivity can be a powerful marketing tool, it must be managed ethically. Ensure that the use of exclusivity does not lead to discrimination or unfair practices. It should enhance consumer experience and value, not exploit consumer insecurities.

Conclusion

The Law of Exclusivity is an effective strategy for enhancing the appeal and demand of products and services. By carefully crafting exclusive offers, you can not only increase desirability and perceived value but also build a loyal customer base that feels privileged and valued. Whether through limited editions, members-only access, or personalized experiences, exclusivity can significantly impact consumer behavior and brand perception.

CHAPTER 30: THE LAW OF SIMPLICITY

Streamlining Communication for Maximum Impact

The Law of Simplicity underscores the importance of clarity and straightforwardness in effective communication. In a world inundated with information, messages that are simple and easy to understand stand out and are more likely to be remembered. Simplicity helps to avoid confusion, reduces cognitive load, and facilitates quicker and more confident decision-making by the audience.

Understanding the Power of Simplicity

Simplicity in communication involves distilling messages to their essential elements and presenting them in an accessible and unambiguous manner. This approach respects the audience's time and cognitive resources, making it easier for them to engage with and act on the information presented.

Key Principles of Effective Simplicity

1. **Clarity of Purpose**: Every message should have a clear and singular focus. This helps to prevent the dilution of the core message and ensures that the audience understands the intended outcome.

2. **Economy of Language**: Use concise language and avoid unnecessary jargon or technical terms that could alienate or confuse the audience. Simplicity in wording helps in making the communication more accessible to a broader audience.

3. **Visual Cleanliness**: In visual communication, simplicity can

be achieved through clean, uncluttered designs that focus on key elements. Visual simplicity aids in drawing attention to the most important information.

4. **Repetition and Reinforcement**: Repeating key points in a simple, consistent manner helps to reinforce the message and aids in retention.

Strategies for Implementing the Law of Simplicity

1. **Prioritize Information**: Identify the most important pieces of information you want to convey and focus on these. Avoid overwhelming the audience with too many details at once.

2. **Break Down Complex Ideas**: When dealing with complex information, break it down into manageable, understandable parts. Use analogies or metaphors to relate new ideas to familiar concepts.

3. **Use Active Voice**: Communicate in an active voice as much as possible. Active voice is direct and easier to understand, making your statements more clear and impactful.

4. **Iterative Simplification**: After crafting your message, review it to see if there are ways to simplify further. This might involve removing redundant elements, using simpler words, or restructuring sentences for clarity.

Applications Across Various Fields

- **Marketing**: In marketing, simple, clear messages are more likely to cut through the noise of competing advertisements and resonate with consumers.

- **Education**: Educators can enhance learning by presenting information in clear, simple stages, helping students to grasp and retain complex subjects more effectively.

- **Technical Communication**: In technical fields, simplifying information without losing accuracy is crucial, especially when communicating safety procedures or product instructions.

Ethical Considerations

While simplicity is valuable, it must not lead to oversimplification that misrepresents the truth or omits critical information. Ensure that simplification does not compromise the accuracy or integrity of the information.

Conclusion

The Law of Simplicity is crucial for effective communication, especially in environments where attention is limited and information overload is common. By keeping messages clear and straightforward, you enhance understanding and engagement, making it easier for your audience to absorb and act on your messages. This approach not only improves the effectiveness of communication but also builds trust and credibility by respecting the audience's need for clarity and precision.

CHAPTER 31: THE LAW OF NOVELTY

Captivating Attention
with Innovation

The Law of Novelty posits that new and innovative ideas naturally capture more attention and stimulate interest. Humans are wired to respond to novelty; it triggers areas of the brain associated with reward and discovery, prompting engagement and exploration. This intrinsic response can be leveraged in various fields to attract interest, drive engagement, and create memorable experiences.

Understanding the Appeal of Novelty

Novelty acts as a cognitive stimulant. When individuals encounter something new, it interrupts the familiarity of their daily routine and triggers a series of neural processes aimed at understanding and integrating this new information. This neurological activity not only heightens attention but also enhances the retention of the novel information, making it a powerful tool for effective communication.

Key Benefits of Leveraging Novelty

1. **Increased Engagement**: Novel stimuli are more likely to stand out from the mundane, drawing in and holding attention.

2. **Enhanced Memory Retention**: The brain tends to prioritize new information for memory storage, which can increase the likelihood that your message or brand remains top-of-mind.

3. **Stimulated Curiosity**: Novelty can spark curiosity, driving

individuals to explore further. This can be particularly beneficial in educational settings or in marketing new products.

Strategies for Implementing the Law of Novelty

1. **Introduce Innovations**: Regularly update your offerings or methods to include new features, technologies, or approaches. Even small innovations can reignite interest and engagement.

2. **Use Surprising Elements**: Incorporate unexpected elements into presentations, advertisements, or communications. Surprises can break the monotony and revive interest in your message.

3. **Vary Content Delivery**: Change how content is delivered by experimenting with new formats or platforms. This could mean using interactive tools in digital marketing or incorporating gamification in educational content.

4. **Create Unique Experiences**: Design experiences that are distinct from what your audience typically encounters. Unique experiences are not only more engaging but are also more likely to be shared, expanding your reach.

Applications Across Various Fields

- **Marketing and Branding**: Brands can introduce novel products or unique marketing campaigns to differentiate themselves from competitors and capture market attention.

- **Education**: Educators can use novel teaching tools or techniques to engage students more effectively, making learning experiences more dynamic and memorable.

- **Product Development**: Companies can incorporate cutting-edge technologies or design elements into new products to make them stand out in crowded markets.

Ethical Considerations

While novelty can be a powerful tool, it's important to ensure that the new elements you introduce are relevant and provide real value. Novelty for its own sake, without underlying substance, can lead to disappointment and damage trust.

Conclusion

The Law of Novelty is a crucial aspect of strategy in any field where keeping an audience's attention and interest is key. By continually incorporating new and innovative elements into your offerings or communications, you can maintain an engaged and enthusiastic audience. This approach not only makes your messages more compelling but also fosters an environment of continual learning and curiosity, driving both growth and loyalty.

CHAPTER 32: THE LAW OF VISIBILITY

*Maximizing Influence Through
Strategic Presence*

T he Law of Visibility emphasizes the importance of being seen regularly in positive contexts to establish a strong presence and influence. Visibility is crucial in shaping perceptions; the more people see you or your brand in contexts that align with positive values and outcomes, the more likely they are to think of you positively and trust your authority. This principle applies to personal branding, marketing, leadership, and virtually any arena where public perception impacts success.

Understanding the Impact of Visibility

Visibility increases familiarity, and familiarity breeds trust and comfort. Being consistently visible in the right contexts helps to cement your image and message in the minds of your audience. It also provides numerous opportunities to display your values, skills, and reliability, which are essential for building lasting influence.

Key Benefits of Enhanced Visibility

1. **Increased Trust and Credibility**: Regular visibility in respected venues or contexts boosts your credibility. People are more likely to believe and support what they are familiar with.

2. **Association with Positive Attributes**: By being seen in positive or aspirational contexts, you naturally inherit some of those positive associations. This can enhance your appeal

and authority.

3. **Top-of-Mind Awareness**: Frequent visibility ensures that you remain at the forefront of your audience's mind, which is particularly important in competitive environments.

Strategies for Implementing the Law of Visibility

1. **Leverage Multiple Platforms**: Utilize various platforms—social media, blogs, public speaking engagements, and publications—to maintain a steady stream of visibility. Each platform reaches different segments of your audience, enhancing your overall presence.

2. **Engage Regularly**: Consistency in engagement is key. Regular updates, posts, and interactions help keep your audience engaged and reinforce your presence.

3. **Participate in Relevant Events**: Align yourself with events and activities that reflect your values and those of your target audience. Whether it's industry conferences, community service, or public forums, your presence at these events strengthens your visibility and credibility.

4. **Collaborate with Respected Peers**: Collaborations can significantly boost visibility. Working with well-respected figures or brands in your industry can also lend additional credibility and extend your reach.

Applications Across Various Fields

- **In Business**: Companies can increase visibility by consistently appearing in industry rankings, engaging in community events, and maintaining an active online presence.

- **In Politics**: Politicians need to be visible in their constituencies and at events that matter to their voters to build and maintain support.

- **In Academia and Thought Leadership**: Regular publications, lectures, and participation in academic forums help build a reputation as a thought leader.

Ethical Considerations

While seeking visibility, it's crucial to maintain authenticity and integrity. Visibility should not be achieved at the cost of misrepresenting your capabilities or engaging in activities that conflict with your core values. Moreover, respect for privacy and boundaries, both yours and others', should always be considered.

Conclusion

The Law of Visibility is a powerful tool for building influence and establishing presence in any field. By strategically enhancing how often and in what contexts you are seen, you can significantly improve your perceived credibility and authority. Effective visibility is not just about being seen; it's about being seen consistently in the right places and in the right ways that align with your goals and values.

CHAPTER 33: THE LAW OF ACKNOWLEDGMENT

Building Connections through Recognition

The Law of Acknowledgment focuses on the importance of recognizing and appreciating others, a key strategy for fostering goodwill and enhancing both collaborative and persuasive efforts. By acknowledging the contributions, feelings, and achievements of others, you create an environment of respect and trust, which are foundational for effective communication and teamwork.

Understanding the Power of Acknowledgment

Acknowledgment validates the efforts and existence of others, signaling that their contributions or feelings are seen and valued. This validation is crucial for building strong relationships, as it meets a fundamental human need for recognition and belonging. When people feel acknowledged, they are more likely to be cooperative, loyal, and motivated.

Key Benefits of Effective Acknowledgment

1. **Enhanced Engagement**: When individuals feel acknowledged, they are more engaged and invested in their tasks. Engagement not only boosts productivity but also fosters a positive atmosphere that can spread throughout an organization or community.

2. **Increased Trust and Openness**: Regular acknowledgment helps build trust, making people more open to sharing ideas and feedback. This openness is crucial for continuous improvement and innovation.

3. **Strengthened Relationships**: By showing appreciation, you strengthen relationships, which are the bedrock of effective teamwork and successful negotiation.

Strategies for Implementing the Law of Acknowledgment

1. **Personalize Your Acknowledgment**: Tailor your recognition to the individual, making it as personal and specific as possible. This shows genuine appreciation and understanding of the individual's unique contribution.

2. **Be Timely and Frequent**: Acknowledgment should be given as soon as possible after the contribution has been made. Frequent recognition reinforces positive behaviors and ensures that individuals consistently feel valued.

3. **Incorporate Public and Private Recognition**: While public recognition can significantly boost morale and serve as a powerful motivator for others, private acknowledgment can be equally important for fostering a deep sense of value and respect.

4. **Use Varied Forms of Acknowledgment**: Acknowledgment can take many forms, from verbal praise and written thank-you notes to awards or tokens of appreciation. Using a variety of forms keeps the recognition fresh and meaningful.

Applications Across Various Fields

- **In Leadership**: Leaders who regularly acknowledge their team's efforts can inspire loyalty and drive, making it easier to achieve group objectives.

- **In Sales and Customer Service**: Recognizing and appreciating customers can enhance brand loyalty and increase customer satisfaction, leading to repeat business and referrals.

- **In Personal Relationships**: Regularly acknowledging the efforts and feelings of friends and family strengthens bonds and enhances mutual respect and support.

Ethical Considerations

Acknowledgment must be genuine and deserved. Inauthentic or manipulative acknowledgment can lead to skepticism and diminish trust. It's important that recognition is based on real achievements or contributions and not used as a mere tool for persuasion.

Conclusion

The Law of Acknowledgment is a potent tool for building positive relationships and fostering an environment of mutual respect and cooperation. By effectively recognizing and appreciating the efforts of others, you not only enhance individual motivation and morale but also create a supportive network that can propel collective success. This approach enriches both personal interactions and professional engagements, making it an essential strategy for anyone looking to enhance their influence and effectiveness.

CHAPTER 34: THE LAW OF LIMITATION

Simplifying Choices to Enhance Decision-Making

The Law of Limitation focuses on the strategic reduction of choices to streamline decision-making and guide individuals towards more effective outcomes. In a world where the abundance of options can lead to paralysis and dissatisfaction, limiting choices can paradoxically enhance freedom by making it easier for people to decide and feel confident about their decisions.

Understanding the Impact of Limited Choices

Excessive choices, though seemingly beneficial, can often overwhelm and lead to decision fatigue, where the quality of decisions deteriorates as a person makes more choices. Furthermore, too many options can increase the likelihood of regret and second-guessing, as individuals wonder if they made the best possible choice. By limiting options, you can reduce these negative effects and guide decisions in a more focused and satisfying direction.

Benefits of Implementing the Law of Limitation

1. **Enhanced Clarity and Ease**: Fewer choices reduce complexity and make it easier for individuals to compare options and make decisions. This can lead to quicker decision-making and increased satisfaction.

2. **Reduced Anxiety and Indecision**: Limiting options can decrease the anxiety associated with making the "perfect" choice, as each option is more likely to be satisfactory.

3. **Increased Perceived Value**: When choices are limited, the available options can seem more valuable, particularly if the selection process is curated to only include high-quality choices.

Strategies for Leveraging the Law of Limitation

1. **Curate Choices Thoughtfully**: When limiting options, ensure that the remaining choices are high-quality and tailored to the needs and preferences of the decision-maker. This involves understanding your audience or customers deeply and anticipating their needs.

2. **Create Clear Categories**: If a large number of options is necessary, organize them into distinct and clear categories. This helps people navigate the choices more easily and reduces the cognitive load by clustering similar items together.

3. **Offer Tiered Options**: Provide options at different levels (such as good, better, best) to cater to different needs or budget levels without overwhelming the decision-maker. This approach simplifies decision-making while still accommodating diverse preferences.

4. **Use Defaults**: Setting defaults can effectively guide choices while still leaving room for personalization. Defaults take advantage of the Law of Limitation by presenting a pre-selected option that most people are likely to stick with, thereby simplifying the decision process.

Applications Across Various Fields

- **Product Design and Retail**: Businesses can streamline their product lines to focus on a limited number of popular or highly effective products, simplifying consumer choice and improving inventory management.

- **Menu Design in Restaurants**: By limiting the number of dishes offered, restaurants can not only improve the quality of each dish but also make it easier for customers to decide what to order.

- **Healthcare and Insurance**: Providing a curated set of healthcare plans or treatment options can help patients make better-informed decisions without feeling overwhelmed by the complexities of the choices.

Ethical Considerations

While limiting choices can simplify decision-making, it is important to ensure that it does not restrict essential freedoms or lead to manipulation. The process of limiting options should be transparent, and the rationale for how and why choices are curated should be clear to those affected.

Conclusion

The Law of Limitation is a powerful principle for improving decision-making efficiency and satisfaction. By judiciously curating and limiting choices, you can help individuals make decisions that are quicker, more satisfying, and more likely to meet their needs. This approach not only enhances individual experiences but also streamlines operations and improves outcomes in various professional and personal contexts.

CHAPTER 35: THE LAW OF POWER

Influencing Through Authority and Confidence

The Law of Power highlights the significant impact that projecting strength and certainty can have on influencing perceptions and shaping outcomes. In various settings, from leadership and negotiation to public speaking and personal interactions, the display of confidence and authority can command respect, sway opinions, and steer decisions. Understanding and mastering this law can elevate one's ability to lead and persuade effectively.

Understanding the Dynamics of Power Projection

Power projection isn't merely about displaying dominance but involves conveying confidence, competence, and authority in a way that inspires trust and admiration. When people perceive someone as powerful, they are more likely to defer to this person's judgments and decisions, assuming that such confidence is backed by expertise and capability.

Benefits of Effective Power Projection

1. **Enhanced Leadership Presence**: Leaders who project power effectively are more likely to be followed and respected. This presence can help in mobilizing teams, driving change, and achieving organizational goals.

2. **Increased Influence in Negotiations**: In negotiations, a strong, confident stance can lead to more favorable outcomes, as it suggests that you have high expectations and firm boundaries.

3. **Greater Persuasive Impact**: People are generally more persuaded by speakers who appear confident and authoritative. This can be particularly beneficial in sales, marketing, and public advocacy.

Strategies for Leveraging the Law of Power

1. **Develop Expertise**: True power often stems from deep expertise. Continuously developing your knowledge and skills in your field can naturally enhance your confidence and authority.

2. **Cultivate a Commanding Presence**: Pay attention to your posture, voice, and demeanor. Standing tall, speaking clearly, and maintaining eye contact can convey confidence and authority.

3. **Communicate Decisively**: Use clear and assertive language. Avoid qualifiers like "I think" or "maybe," which can undermine your statements. Instead, speak in definitive terms when appropriate.

4. **Practice Emotional Stability**: Being able to maintain composure, especially in challenging situations, projects strength and control, reinforcing your power in the eyes of others.

5. **Use Social Proof**: Highlight your past successes and endorsements from credible sources. This not only builds your reputation but also solidifies your authority in your current interactions.

Applications Across Various Fields

- **Organizational Leadership**: Executives and managers can use power projection to inspire confidence among stakeholders and drive forward corporate strategies.

- **Political Leadership**: Politicians need to project strength and certainty to garner support and lead effectively, particularly in times of crisis.

- **Public Speaking**: Speakers who project confidence can engage and persuade their audiences more effectively, making their messages more compelling and memorable.

Ethical Considerations

While projecting power can be highly effective, it must be balanced with ethical considerations. Misusing power or displaying arrogance can lead to negative outcomes, including loss of trust and respect. It's important to combine strength with empathy and humility to ensure that your influence is both positive and sustainable.

Conclusion

The Law of Power is a pivotal aspect of influence, shaping how individuals perceive you and respond to your leadership or message. By projecting strength and certainty thoughtfully and ethically, you can enhance your leadership presence, influence outcomes in negotiations, and make your communications more persuasive. This approach not only advances your objectives but also inspires and motivates those around you.

CHAPTER 36: THE LAW OF URGENCY

Driving Action Through Timely Stimuli

The Law of Urgency highlights the effectiveness of creating a sense of urgency to spur people into immediate action. This principle leverages the natural human tendency to prioritize tasks that appear time-sensitive or urgent. By effectively invoking urgency, you can increase the likelihood of prompt decisions and actions, which is particularly useful in sales, negotiations, and situations requiring quick response.

Understanding the Psychological Basis of Urgency

Urgency works by tapping into the human psychological response to perceived scarcity and time constraints. When people believe that an opportunity is limited in time, they are more likely to act quickly to avoid missing out. This response is driven by both the fear of loss (loss aversion) and the desire to secure a perceived benefit while it is still available.

Benefits of Cultivating Urgency

1. **Increased Engagement and Attention**: Urgency captures and holds attention, as people prioritize tasks that they perceive as time-sensitive.

2. **Accelerated Decision-Making**: Urgency can reduce procrastination and deliberation, prompting quicker decision-making processes.

3. **Enhanced Conversion Rates**: In marketing and sales, urgency

can drive higher conversion rates as customers are more likely to complete purchases immediately rather than delaying.

Strategies for Leveraging the Law of Urgency

1. **Clear Deadlines**: Establish clear and visible deadlines for offers or decisions. This can be done through countdown timers on websites, last-minute registration alerts for events, or limited-time sales promotions.

2. **Limited Quantities**: Highlight the limited availability of an offer. Phrases like "only a few left in stock" or "limited seats available" create a sense of urgency due to the scarcity of the opportunity.

3. **Exclusive Offers**: Present offers as exclusive or available only to a select group of customers for a limited time. This not only utilizes urgency but also combines it with the allure of exclusivity.

4. **Immediate Benefits**: Emphasize the immediate benefits of taking action now. For instance, outline the advantages that come with an immediate purchase or decision, such as instant savings or immediate access to products or services.

Applications Across Various Fields

- **Marketing and Retail**: Businesses use urgency to drive sales during promotions by indicating that discounts will end soon or that there is a limited stock of popular items.

- **Nonprofit and Fundraising**: Urgency is employed in fundraising campaigns by setting a deadline for donations, especially when approaching fiscal year-end or during specific fundraising events.

- **Emergency Services**: In critical services, communicating urgency can ensure that immediate actions are taken in response to emergencies, enhancing the effectiveness of responses.

Ethical Considerations

While the Law of Urgency is powerful, it must be used ethically. Creating false urgency (such as fabricating limited offers or deadlines) can lead to consumer distrust and damage a brand's reputation. Therefore, it's crucial that any use of urgency is genuine and transparent.

Conclusion

The Law of Urgency is a critical tool for inducing immediate action and can greatly enhance outcomes in sales, marketing, and any field where timely response is crucial. By understanding and applying this law, you can motivate faster decision-making and increase engagement, but it should always be implemented with honesty and integrity to maintain trust and credibility.

CHAPTER 37: THE LAW OF PATIENCE

Cultivating Influence Through Time

The Law of Patience emphasizes the significance of allowing time for influence and relationships to develop organically. In a world often focused on immediate results, understanding the value of patience can be a strategic advantage. Long-term strategies in persuasion and relationship-building often yield more sustainable and impactful outcomes, as they allow for trust and credibility to grow deeper with time.

Understanding the Dynamics of Patience

Patience in persuasion and relationship-building involves more than merely waiting; it's about strategically nurturing connections, allowing ideas to mature, and understanding that some processes cannot be rushed without compromising their quality or depth. Patience demonstrates respect for the natural development of trust and ideas, which can lead to more meaningful and enduring influence.

Benefits of Employing the Law of Patience

1. **Deeper Trust**: Trust built slowly over time tends to be more resilient and enduring. Patience allows you to demonstrate consistency and reliability, which are key components of trust.

2. **Richer Relationships**: Relationships nurtured over time allow for a deeper understanding of the other party's needs, desires, and personality. This depth can make your persuasive efforts more tailored and effective.

3. **Enhanced Credibility**: Taking time to develop your ideas or

arguments fully can enhance your credibility. Rushed ideas are often less polished and can be perceived as less thoughtful or thorough.

Strategies for Implementing the Law of Patience

1. **Set Realistic Expectations**: Communicate realistic timelines and manage expectations, both your own and those of others involved. This helps prevent frustration and maintains motivation.

2. **Consistent Engagement**: Regularly engage with your audience or stakeholders in meaningful ways. Consistency shows commitment and helps keep the relationship or dialogue alive, even if progress seems slow.

3. **Responsive Adaptation**: While being patient, stay responsive to changes and feedback. Adaptation shows that you are attentive and committed to continuous improvement, not just biding time.

4. **Celebrate Small Wins**: Recognize and celebrate progress along the way. This keeps morale high and demonstrates the value of the incremental efforts that contribute to the larger goal.

Applications Across Various Fields

- **Business Development**: Long-term client relationships are vital in industries where trust is crucial, such as financial services or consulting. Patience in building these relationships can lead to more significant contracts and loyal clients.

- **Marketing**: Building a brand takes time. Effective brand strategies require patience as the market's awareness and loyalty gradually increase.

- **Personal Growth and Education**: Learning and personal development are inherently gradual processes. Patience is essential to achieving deep expertise and skill in any field.

Ethical Considerations

Patience should not lead to complacency or inaction. It's important to differentiate between patiently waiting for the right moment and missing opportunities due to indecision. Similarly, patience should not be used as an excuse for tolerating poor performance or harmful behaviors.

Conclusion

The Law of Patience is a powerful tool in building lasting influence and relationships. By understanding and valuing the role of time in the development of trust and ideas, you can implement strategies that yield more substantial and lasting results. Patience not only enhances the quality of outcomes but also strengthens the bonds between all parties involved, leading to more fruitful and sustainable success.

CHAPTER 38: THE LAW
OF DEMONSTRATION

Enhancing Persuasion
through Active Proof

The Law of Demonstration emphasizes the persuasive power of showing concrete examples and evidence rather than merely telling about them. Demonstrating the value of an idea, product, or service through tangible examples, live demonstrations, or compelling testimonials can significantly increase credibility and influence the decision-making process more effectively than abstract descriptions.

Understanding the Effectiveness of Demonstrations

Demonstrations provide sensory experience or visual proof that can validate claims and make abstract concepts concrete. When people witness a product in action or see the results firsthand, their doubts diminish, and their understanding deepens. This direct experience often resonates more powerfully than verbal explanations or written descriptions alone.

Key Benefits of the Law of Demonstration

1. **Enhanced Credibility**: Demonstrations showcase your confidence in your product or idea and validate its effectiveness, enhancing your credibility.

2. **Increased Engagement**: Interactive or visual demonstrations are more engaging than passive descriptions. They capture attention and encourage a deeper interaction with the content.

3. **Emotional Connection**: Seeing a product in action or hearing

a testimonial can evoke emotional responses that are likely to influence buying decisions more effectively than features and specifications.

Strategies for Implementing the Law of Demonstration

1. **Use Visual Aids**: Whenever possible, use visuals such as charts, videos, prototypes, or live feeds to demonstrate your points. Visual aids help clarify complex information and make your message more memorable.

2. **Incorporate Testimonials and Case Studies**: Share stories and testimonials from real users who have benefited from your product or service. Real-world examples can be very compelling, especially if they are relatable to your audience.

3. **Offer Live Demonstrations**: In settings such as trade shows, retail environments, or during presentations, live demonstrations allow potential customers or stakeholders to see exactly how something works, enhancing transparency and trust.

4. **Provide Free Trials or Samples**: Allowing customers to experience your product firsthand can dramatically boost conversion rates. Free trials and samples reduce risk for the user, thereby enhancing the appeal of your offer.

5. **Create Comparison Scenarios**: Showcasing your product or service alongside competitors' can highlight its advantages effectively. This direct comparison can solidify the perceived value of your offerings.

Applications Across Various Fields

- **Marketing and Sales**: Product demonstrations in stores or at trade shows can directly influence purchase decisions by highlighting functionality and benefits firsthand.

- **Education and Training**: Using practical demonstrations in educational settings can help students understand and remember concepts better by linking theory with practice.

- **Technology and Software**: Providing demos or limited-time access to software allows users to experience functionality directly, which can be crucial for complex or high-value products.

Ethical Considerations

While demonstrations are powerful, they must accurately represent what you are selling or promoting. Misleading demonstrations that exaggerate capabilities or results can lead to dissatisfaction and damage your reputation.

Conclusion

The Law of Demonstration is a critical strategy in persuasion that leverages the power of seeing to believe. By effectively demonstrating the value of your ideas, products, or services, you can enhance understanding, credibility, and emotional engagement, leading to more informed and enthusiastic responses from your audience. This approach not only supports clearer communication but also builds trust and confidence in your offerings.

CHAPTER 39: THE LAW OF TESTIMONIALS

Boosting Credibility with Endorsements

The Law of Testaments highlights the significant impact that endorsements and testimonials from credible sources can have on enhancing persuasive efforts. Whether it's promoting a product, service, or idea, leveraging the voices of satisfied customers or respected figures can substantially increase trust and legitimacy in the eyes of potential clients or stakeholders.

Understanding the Impact of Testimonials

Testimonials and endorsements work by providing social proof, a psychological phenomenon where people assume the actions and opinions of others reflect correct behavior. When potential customers see that others—especially those they admire or trust—approve of a product or service, their own confidence in that offering increases. This is particularly effective when the endorsements come from credible, respected sources that the audience can relate to or aspires to emulate.

Key Benefits of Using Testimonials

1. **Enhanced Trust**: Testimonials from real users or respected experts help to build trust more quickly than promotional content alone, as they are perceived as less biased and more authentic.

2. **Increased Relatability**: Seeing or hearing from real users who have benefited from a product or service makes it easier for potential customers to envision themselves having similar

positive experiences.

3. **Elevated Authority**: Endorsements from industry experts or celebrities can lend an air of authority and prestige, making the product or service seem more desirable.

Strategies for Leveraging the Law of Testimonials

1. **Choose Relevant Testimonials**: Ensure that the testimonials you use are relevant to your target audience. They should address specific concerns or desires that resonate with potential customers.

2. **Diversify Your Sources**: Including a range of testimonials from different demographics and backgrounds can broaden the appeal of your product or service, making it relatable to a wider audience.

3. **Incorporate Various Formats**: Testimonials can be presented in different formats, including written quotes, video interviews, case studies, and social media posts. Using a variety of formats can cater to different preferences and increase engagement.

4. **Highlight Specific Benefits**: Rather than general praise, encourage your endorsers to speak about specific benefits they experienced. Detailed testimonials can be more persuasive and informative for potential users.

5. **Use Ethically and Transparently**: Always obtain permission to use someone's testimonial, and ensure that the endorsements are truthful and not misleading. Transparency about whether endorsers have been compensated is also crucial to maintain trust.

Applications Across Various Fields

- **Marketing and Sales**: Businesses can feature customer testimonials in advertising campaigns, on websites, and in promotional materials to increase conversions and sales.

- **Non-Profit Organizations**: Non-profits can use testimonials from beneficiaries to show the impact of their work and encourage donations and support.

- **Healthcare**: Patient testimonials can be effective in healthcare marketing, as they help to alleviate concerns by showing real outcomes.

- **Corporate Training and Education**: Testimonials from past participants can enhance the perceived value of training programs and workshops, encouraging more sign-ups.

Conclusion

The Law of Testimonials is a powerful tool in persuasion, offering a way to showcase the real-world value and satisfaction of a product or service. By strategically utilizing testimonials and endorsements, you can significantly enhance the credibility and appeal of your offerings, fostering trust and confidence that drives decision-making.

CHAPTER 40: THE LAW OF TENSION

Harnessing Dynamic Tension for Motivation

T he Law of Tension explores the concept of using carefully managed tension to motivate action and influence decisions. Dynamic tension, in this context, refers to the psychological strain experienced when there is a gap between a current state and a desired outcome. By effectively creating and maintaining this tension without causing distress, you can spur individuals towards taking action to resolve the tension.

Understanding the Role of Tension

Dynamic tension is a powerful motivator because it creates a sense of urgency and necessity. It is closely related to goal-setting theory, where the tension between the current reality and the envisioned goal drives people to engage in activities that will reduce this disparity. The key to utilizing tension effectively is to strike the right balance—enough to motivate but not so much as to overwhelm.

Benefits of Employing the Law of Tension

1. **Increased Engagement**: Tension can capture and hold attention. People are naturally inclined to resolve uncertainties, making them more engaged with the situation or task at hand.

2. **Enhanced Motivation**: The desire to relieve tension can lead to increased motivation. When individuals see clear steps to resolve the tension, they are more likely to take action.

3. **Improved Problem-Solving**: Tension often encourages creative thinking and problem-solving as individuals seek ways to alleviate the discomfort it causes.

Strategies for Leveraging the Law of Tension

1. **Set Clear, Challenging Goals**: Establish goals that are ambitious yet achievable. The gap between the current situation and the goal creates a natural tension that urges progress.

2. **Provide Partial Information**: Reveal information in stages to maintain curiosity and engagement. This method keeps individuals invested in "finding out more," maintaining an ongoing tension.

3. **Use Conflict Effectively**: Introduce elements of conflict, such as competing interests or challenging obstacles, that require active resolution. This type of tension can drive teams to collaborate more closely and seek innovative solutions.

4. **Create Scenarios of High Stakes**: Communicate the high stakes involved in achieving or failing to achieve the goals. When the consequences of inaction are significant, the tension created can push individuals towards decisive action.

Applications Across Various Fields

- **Marketing and Advertising**: Marketers often create campaigns that highlight what consumers stand to lose if they do not act, such as limited-time offers or exclusive deals that won't last.

- **Organizational Change Management**: In managing change within organizations, leaders can use tension by clearly outlining the dangers of the status quo versus the benefits of change.

- **Education**: Educators can use tension by setting high standards and challenging students to reach them, thereby motivating greater effort and engagement.

Ethical Considerations

While using tension can be effective, it is important to manage it ethically. Excessive tension can lead to stress, burnout, and a negative atmosphere. It's crucial to monitor and adjust the level of tension to ensure it remains a positive and motivating force.

Conclusion

The Law of Tension, when managed properly, can be an extremely effective tool in driving action and encouraging decision-making. By creating a gap between the current state and a desirable outcome, and by carefully managing the steps to bridge this gap, you can motivate individuals and groups to engage deeply and act decisively.

CHAPTER 41: THE LAW OF SILENCE

Enhancing Influence Through Strategic Silence

The Law of Silence underscores the power of choosing when and what not to say, illustrating that sometimes, saying less can indeed be more influential. Strategic silence can enhance the impact of messages, create intrigue, encourage others to reveal more, and allow time for the information presented to be absorbed and considered. In various communication settings, understanding how to effectively employ silence can significantly strengthen your influence.

Understanding the Effectiveness of Silence

Silence, used judiciously, can serve multiple functions in communication:

1. **Creates Space for Reflection**: Allowing pauses after key points gives the audience time to think about what has been said, potentially leading to deeper understanding and retention.

2. **Builds Suspense and Interest**: Strategic silence can create suspense and anticipation, making the audience more eager to hear what will come next.

3. **Signals Confidence and Control**: Demonstrating comfort with silence can convey confidence and authority, suggesting mastery over the subject matter and self-assuredness.

Benefits of Employing the Law of Silent

1. **Enhanced Message Clarity**: By not overcrowding your speech with excessive words, the key messages stand out more clearly to the audience.

2. **Increased Perceived Wisdom**: Individuals who speak less but with thoughtful content are often perceived as more reflective and wise.

3. **Improved Listening**: Silence can encourage others to speak, providing you with more information and a better understanding of their perspectives, which is particularly useful in negotiations and conflict resolution.

Strategies for Leveraging the Law of Silence

1. **Pause for Emphasis**: After making an important point, pause to let it resonate. This not only highlights the significance of what was said but also gives listeners time to formulate thoughts and questions.

2. **Control the Tempo**: Use silence to control the pace of the conversation. Slowing down the flow through strategic pauses can help in managing the direction and dynamics of the dialogue.

3. **Encourage Dialogue**: Sometimes, staying silent after asking a question or presenting a challenge can compel others to fill the silence, often revealing more than they intended or providing valuable insights.

4. **Avoid Filler Words**: Practice speaking without using filler words that can diliter the strength of your messages. This sharpens your speech and makes your silences more powerful.

Applications Across Various Fields

- **Leadership and Management**: Leaders can use silence to empower others, giving them the space to express ideas or take ownership of tasks, which can foster independence and initiative.

- **Negotiations**: In negotiations, silence can be used to put pressure on the other party, often leading them to offer concessions or reveal their negotiation limits.

- **Public Speaking**: Effective public speakers use pauses to strengthen the impact of their words, to emphasize points, and to keep the audience engaged.

Ethical Considerations

While strategic silence can be a powerful tool, it should be used ethically and considerately. Misusing silence to manipulate or coerce can damage trust and undermine relationships. It is essential to balance silence with open and honest communication to maintain integrity and respect in interactions.

Conclusion

The Law of Silence is a subtle yet potent aspect of effective communication. By mastering the art of when and how to remain silent, you can enhance the impact of your words, manage the dynamics of conversations more effectively, and foster an environment where thoughtful communication and deep understanding are prioritized.

CHAPTER 42: THE LAW OF EXPOSURE

Building Comfort and Trust Through Repetition

The Law of Exposure emphasizes that repeated exposure to an idea, product, or person can build familiarity, comfort, and trust, thereby aiding persuasion. This principle, often referred to as the "mere exposure effect," suggests that people tend to develop a preference for things simply because they are familiar with them. By strategically increasing exposure, you can make your message more acceptable and appealing over time.

Understanding the Mere Exposure Effect

The mere exposure effect is a psychological phenomenon where people develop a preference for things they encounter repeatedly. This happens because familiarity reduces uncertainty and perceived risk, making the familiar option seem safer and more trustworthy. The more frequently people are exposed to something, the more likely they are to form a positive attitude towards it, even if initially they had no strong feelings about it.

Benefits of Increased Exposure

1. **Enhanced Trust**: Familiarity breeds trust. Repeated exposure makes an entity appear more reliable and less risky, which is crucial for building trust.

2. **Greater Recall and Recognition**: Repetition aids memory retention, making it more likely that people will remember your message when making decisions.

3. **Increased Likability**: As people become more familiar with something, they tend to find it more likable and agreeable.

Strategies for Leveraging the Law of Exposure

1. **Consistent Branding**: Maintain a consistent presence across various platforms and mediums. This could include advertising, social media, public relations, and direct marketing. The key is to ensure that your audience frequently encounters your brand or message in their daily lives.

2. **Regular Communication**: Engage with your audience regularly through newsletters, blogs, social media updates, or events. Regular communication helps keep your message top-of-mind.

3. **Content Marketing**: Provide valuable content that encourages repeated engagement. This could include articles, videos, podcasts, and other forms of content that draw your audience back repeatedly.

4. **Networking and Public Presence**: Attend industry events, participate in community activities, and be visible in public forums. Personal interactions can significantly enhance familiarity and trust.

5. **Retargeting Campaigns**: In digital marketing, use retargeting strategies to keep your message in front of those who have previously shown interest. This repeated exposure can help convert interest into action.

Applications Across Various Fields

- **Marketing and Sales**: Brands use repeated exposure through advertising campaigns, social media, and content marketing to build brand recognition and loyalty.

- **Politics**: Political candidates often increase their exposure through media appearances, advertisements, and public events to become familiar and trustworthy to voters.

- **Education**: Repetition of key concepts and ideas in

educational settings helps students retain and understand the material better.

- **Personal Relationships**: Regular interactions and consistent communication are crucial in building and maintaining trust in personal relationships.

Ethical Considerations

While the mere exposure effect can be powerful, it should be used ethically. Overexposure or manipulative use of repeated exposure can lead to irritation and distrust. It is important to balance frequency with quality and ensure that each interaction or exposure adds value to the audience.

Conclusion

The Law of Exposure is a fundamental principle in building familiarity, comfort, and trust. By strategically increasing the frequency of exposure to your message, you can enhance its acceptance and appeal. This approach not only aids in persuasion but also fosters a deeper connection and loyalty with your audience, ultimately leading to more effective and sustainable influence.

CHAPTER 43: THE
LAW OF VALUE

Maximizing Influence Through
Tangible Benefits

T he Law of Value underscores the critical importance of offering clear, tangible value in any persuasive effort. Whether you're selling a product, presenting an idea, or advocating for a cause, ensuring that your audience perceives concrete benefits is essential for gaining their support and commitment. Value must be explicit, relevant, and compelling to effectively persuade others.

Understanding the Concept of Value

Value refers to the perceived benefit or advantage that your audience gains from your offering. This can take various forms, including financial savings, time efficiency, enhanced well-being, or improved knowledge. The key is to communicate these benefits clearly and ensure they resonate with the specific needs and desires of your audience.

Key Benefits of Offering Clear Value

1. **Enhanced Persuasiveness**: Clear value propositions make it easier for your audience to justify their decisions and actions.

2. **Increased Trust**: Providing tangible value builds trust and credibility, as it shows you are genuinely committed to benefiting your audience.

3. **Higher Engagement and Loyalty**: When people perceive high value, they are more likely to engage deeply and remain loyal over time.

Strategies for Leveraging the Law of Value

1. **Identify and Articulate Benefits**: Clearly identify the benefits of your product, service, or idea. Articulate these benefits in terms that are specific, concrete, and relevant to your audience's needs.

2. **Use Testimonials and Case Studies**: Provide evidence of value through testimonials and case studies. Real-world examples of how others have benefited can significantly enhance your credibility and appeal.

3. **Offer Demonstrations or Free Trials**: Allowing your audience to experience the value firsthand through demonstrations or free trials can be a powerful way to showcase the tangible benefits.

4. **Highlight Unique Selling Points (USPs)**: Emphasize what sets your offering apart from competitors. Your unique selling points should align with what your audience values most.

5. **Provide Clear ROI**: When applicable, clearly outline the return on investment (ROI). This is especially important in business contexts where financial value is a primary consideration.

Applications Across Various Fields

- **Marketing and Sales**: Effective marketing campaigns highlight the unique benefits of products and services, making the value proposition clear and compelling to potential customers.

- **Education**: Educators can enhance student engagement by clearly outlining the practical applications and benefits of the material being taught.

- **Nonprofit and Advocacy**: Nonprofits can attract more donors and volunteers by clearly demonstrating the impact and benefits of their work.

- **Corporate Communication**: In internal communications,

emphasizing the value of initiatives and policies can increase employee buy-in and participation.

Ethical Considerations

While it is important to emphasize value, it must be done honestly and transparently. Exaggerating or misrepresenting the benefits can lead to disappointment and damage your credibility. Always ensure that the value you promise is deliverable and aligned with your audience's expectations.

Conclusion

The Law of Value is a cornerstone of effective persuasion. By consistently offering and communicating clear, tangible value, you can significantly enhance your influence and effectiveness. This approach not only persuades but also builds lasting trust and loyalty, ensuring that your audience remains engaged and committed to your cause, product, or idea.

CHAPTER 44: THE LAW OF RARITY

Enhancing Appeal Through Unique Benefits

The Law of Rarity emphasizes that highlighting the unique benefits of a proposition can significantly set it apart from others and enhance its appeal. In a crowded marketplace of ideas, products, and services, what stands out are those offerings that possess distinctive attributes. Emphasizing these unique characteristics not only differentiates your proposition but also makes it more desirable and memorable.

Understanding the Power of Rarity

Rarity creates a perception of exclusivity and value. When something is unique or scarce, it becomes more attractive because it implies that it offers something special that cannot be easily found elsewhere. This scarcity principle is deeply rooted in human psychology, where the desire for rare items is often driven by a fear of missing out and the allure of possessing something exceptional.

Key Benefits of Emphasizing Rarity

1. **Increased Perceived Value**: Unique benefits enhance the perceived value of a proposition. When people believe they are getting something special, they are more likely to value and invest in it.

2. **Greater Competitive Edge**: Differentiating your offering from others in the market gives you a competitive edge, making it easier to capture attention and interest.

3. **Enhanced Memorability**: Unique propositions are more memorable. When your offering stands out, it is more likely to be remembered and recommended.

Strategies for Leveraging the Law of Rarity

1. **Identify Unique Selling Points (USPs)**: Clearly define what makes your proposition unique. Focus on aspects that cannot be easily replicated by competitors and that address specific needs or desires of your audience.

2. **Communicate Exclusivity**: Use language and visuals that convey exclusivity. Phrases like "limited edition," "exclusive offer," or "one-of-a-kind" can enhance the perception of rarity.

3. **Highlight Unique Features and Benefits**: Make sure to prominently feature the unique attributes of your proposition in all marketing and communication efforts. This can include specialized functions, unique design elements, or rare materials.

4. **Create Limited Availability**: Sometimes, artificially limiting availability can increase perceived rarity and desirability. This can be done through limited-time offers, limited production runs, or exclusive memberships.

5. **Leverage Storytelling**: Use storytelling to highlight the uniqueness of your proposition. Stories about the creation process, the inspiration behind it, or its special impact can make it stand out.

Applications Across Various Fields

- **Luxury Goods**: High-end brands often emphasize rarity by producing limited quantities and using unique materials, thereby enhancing their allure and justifying premium prices.

- **Technology and Innovation**: Tech companies highlight unique features or cutting-edge advancements that set their products apart from the competition.

- **Art and Entertainment**: Artists and entertainers emphasize the uniqueness of their work or performances to create a dedicated following and command higher value.

- **Education and Training**: Educational institutions and trainers can differentiate their programs by offering specialized courses or unique teaching methodologies that are not widely available.

Ethical Considerations

While emphasizing rarity can be effective, it should be done ethically. Misleading claims about exclusivity or creating false scarcity can lead to distrust and damage your reputation. Ensure that the unique benefits you promote are genuine and verifiable.

Conclusion

The Law of Rarity is a powerful principle for enhancing the appeal and value of a proposition. By identifying and emphasizing unique benefits, you can effectively differentiate your offering, making it more attractive and memorable to your audience. This approach not only captures attention but also fosters a sense of exclusivity and desirability, driving higher engagement and commitment.

CHAPTER 45: THE LAW OF TRANSPARENCY

Building Trust Through Openness and Honesty

T he Law of Transparency highlights the critical role of openness and honesty in building trust and facilitating influence. In an era where information is readily accessible, and consumers are more informed and skeptical than ever, transparency has become a cornerstone of effective communication and leadership. By being transparent, you not only build trust but also foster deeper connections and more sustainable influence.

Understanding the Importance of Transparency

Transparency involves being open about intentions, processes, and outcomes. It means providing clear, truthful information and being upfront about any limitations, risks, or uncertainties. When people feel that they are getting the full picture, they are more likely to trust and engage with you or your organization.

Key Benefits of Emphasizing Transparency

1. **Enhanced Trust**: Trust is the foundation of any successful relationship, whether personal or professional. Transparency helps build and maintain this trust by ensuring that there are no hidden agendas or surprises.

2. **Improved Relationships**: Open communication fosters stronger, more authentic relationships. People appreciate honesty and are more likely to reciprocate with loyalty and support.

3. **Increased Accountability**: Transparency holds you accountable for your actions and decisions. This accountability can enhance your credibility and reputation.

Strategies for Leveraging the Law of Transparency

1. **Be Honest and Clear**: Always provide honest information, even when it's difficult. Clear communication about what you can and cannot do builds credibility.

2. **Share Information Proactively**: Don't wait for questions or concerns to arise. Share relevant information proactively, keeping your audience informed and engaged.

3. **Admit Mistakes and Limitations**: Acknowledge when things go wrong and take responsibility for mistakes. Admitting limitations and being open about challenges demonstrates integrity.

4. **Provide Insights into Decision-Making**: Explain the rationale behind your decisions and actions. This transparency helps others understand your perspective and trust your judgment.

5. **Encourage Open Dialogue**: Foster an environment where questions and feedback are welcomed. Open dialogue ensures that concerns are addressed promptly and transparently.

Applications Across Various Fields

- **Business and Leadership**: Transparent leaders build stronger, more cohesive teams. By sharing company goals, challenges, and successes, they foster a culture of trust and collaboration.

- **Marketing and Sales**: Brands that are open about their processes, ingredients, sourcing, and business practices tend to attract more loyal customers who appreciate honesty.

- **Public Relations**: In PR, transparency is crucial for managing reputation and handling crises. Being open and truthful with the public can mitigate negative impacts and rebuild trust.

• **Healthcare**: Transparency in healthcare, such as clear communication about treatment options and risks, builds trust between patients and providers and leads to better health outcomes.

Ethical Considerations

Transparency should not be used as a superficial tactic but should stem from genuine commitment to honesty and integrity. Misleading or selectively transparent practices can backfire, leading to a loss of trust and credibility. It's crucial to balance transparency with privacy and confidentiality where appropriate.

Conclusion

The Law of Transparency is a fundamental principle for building trust and facilitating influence. By embracing openness and honesty, you create a foundation of trust that enhances relationships, drives engagement, and fosters long-term success. In an age where authenticity is highly valued, transparency is not just a strategic advantage—it's a necessity for effective communication and leadership.

CHAPTER 46: THE LAW OF DETAILS

Establishing Credibility Through Attention to Detail

The Law of Details emphasizes the critical role that meticulous attention to detail plays in establishing credibility and enhancing persuasive effectiveness. In any endeavor, whether it's presenting an idea, selling a product, or managing a project, the small details can significantly impact perceptions and outcomes. Attention to detail demonstrates professionalism, thoroughness, and care, all of which are crucial for building trust and influence.

Understanding the Power of Details

Details matter because they contribute to the overall impression and effectiveness of your communication or offering. They can differentiate between success and failure, especially in competitive environments. Attention to detail reflects a commitment to quality and excellence, which can significantly enhance your credibility and persuasive power.

Key Benefits of Focusing on Details

1. **Enhanced Credibility**: Demonstrating thoroughness and accuracy builds credibility. People are more likely to trust and respect those who pay attention to details.

2. **Improved Quality and Professionalism**: Attention to detail ensures that your work is polished and professional, which can positively influence perceptions and outcomes.

3. **Reduced Errors and Misunderstandings**: By focusing

on details, you minimize the risk of errors and misunderstandings, leading to more effective communication and execution.

Strategies for Leveraging the Law of Details

1. **Double-Check Information**: Always verify facts, figures, and details before presenting them. Accuracy is fundamental to credibility.

2. **Use Precise Language**: Choose your words carefully and avoid vague or ambiguous language. Precision in communication helps convey your message clearly and effectively.

3. **Prepare Thoroughly**: Whether it's a presentation, a report, or a product launch, thorough preparation ensures that all details are considered and addressed.

4. **Review and Edit**: Take the time to review and edit your work meticulously. Attention to spelling, grammar, formatting, and consistency can significantly enhance the professionalism of your output.

5. **Pay Attention to Aesthetics**: In visual presentations, design, and branding, attention to aesthetics and layout can enhance the clarity and appeal of your message.

Applications Across Various Fields

- **Business and Leadership**: Leaders who pay attention to details are often seen as more competent and trustworthy. Detailed planning and execution can lead to better project outcomes and higher team morale.

- **Marketing and Sales**: In marketing materials, attention to detail in design, copy, and data can enhance credibility and effectiveness. Detailed product descriptions and high-quality visuals can influence purchasing decisions.

- **Education**: Educators who provide detailed feedback and meticulously prepare their lessons can enhance student learning and engagement.

- **Healthcare**: In healthcare, attention to detail in patient care, documentation, and treatment plans is crucial for ensuring patient safety and positive outcomes.

Ethical Considerations

While attention to detail is important, it should not lead to unnecessary perfectionism or micromanagement, which can stifle creativity and productivity. It's essential to balance detail orientation with a broader perspective to ensure overall effectiveness and well-being.

Conclusion

The Law of Details is a vital principle for establishing credibility and enhancing persuasive effectiveness. By meticulously attending to details, you demonstrate professionalism, build trust, and create high-quality outputs that resonate with your audience. Whether in communication, leadership, marketing, or any other field, a focus on details can significantly enhance your influence and success.

CHAPTER 47: THE LAW OF CONCESSION

Maximizing Negotiation Success Through Strategic Concessions

The Law of Concession highlights the strategic use of making concessions that cost little but mean a lot to the other party in negotiations. Concessions can be powerful tools to build goodwill, foster cooperation, and achieve favorable outcomes. By carefully identifying and offering concessions that hold significant value to the other party while having minimal impact on your own position, you can facilitate smoother negotiations and enhance your influence.

Understanding the Role of Concessions in Negotiations

Concessions serve as signals of flexibility and willingness to cooperate. When used effectively, they can break deadlocks, build trust, and create a positive negotiation atmosphere. The key is to make concessions that are perceived as valuable by the other party but do not significantly compromise your own goals or interests.

Key Benefits of Strategic Concessions

1. **Building Goodwill and Trust**: Offering concessions demonstrates a willingness to compromise, which can build goodwill and trust between negotiating parties.

2. **Creating Reciprocity**: Concessions can trigger a sense of reciprocity, prompting the other party to make concessions in return.

3. **Facilitating Agreement**: By addressing specific needs or

concerns of the other party, concessions can help move negotiations towards a mutually satisfactory agreement.

Strategies for Leveraging the Law of Concession

1. **Identify Low-Cost, High-Value Concessions**: Understand what the other party values most and identify concessions that are inexpensive or easy for you to provide but hold significant value for them.

2. **Time Your Concessions**: Offer concessions at strategic points in the negotiation to build momentum and encourage reciprocal concessions. Early concessions can set a cooperative tone, while later concessions can help close deals.

3. **Communicate the Value of Concessions**: Clearly communicate the value of your concessions to ensure they are recognized and appreciated by the other party. This enhances their impact and fosters reciprocity.

4. **Use Concessions to Gain Leverage**: Offer concessions that align with your negotiation goals. For example, offering a concession in one area can help you gain leverage in another area that is more critical to your interests.

5. **Balance Concessions with Firmness**: While making concessions, also maintain a firm stance on your core interests and priorities. This balance shows flexibility without compromising your essential objectives.

Applications Across Various Fields

- **Business Negotiations**: In business deals, offering concessions such as extended payment terms, additional services, or small discounts can facilitate agreements without significantly impacting profitability.

- **Diplomacy and International Relations**: Diplomatic negotiations often involve strategic concessions, such as easing trade restrictions or providing aid, to build alliances and foster cooperation between countries.

- **Workplace and Labor Relations**: In labor negotiations,

employers might offer concessions such as flexible working hours or additional benefits to address employee concerns and reach agreements.

- **Sales and Customer Relations**: Sales professionals can use concessions, like free trials or extended warranties, to close deals and build customer loyalty.

Ethical Considerations

While strategic concessions can be highly effective, they should be used ethically and genuinely. Avoid making insincere concessions or using them to manipulate the other party. Transparency and fairness are crucial for maintaining trust and fostering long-term relationships.

Conclusion

The Law of Concession is a powerful tool for enhancing negotiation success. By strategically offering concessions that cost little but mean a lot to the other party, you can build goodwill, foster cooperation, and achieve favorable outcomes. This approach not only facilitates smoother negotiations but also strengthens relationships and enhances your influence in various negotiation contexts.

CHAPTER 48: THE LAW
OF EXPECTANCY

Shaping Outcomes Through
Positive Anticipation

T he Law of Expectancy explores the power of operating
with positive expectations and how these expectations
can influence and shape outcomes. The principle of
expectancy posits that people's attitudes and behaviors are
often aligned with what they anticipate. By maintaining an
optimistic outlook, you can influence not only your own actions
and attitudes but also those of others, creating a self-fulfilling
prophecy that drives positive results.

Understanding the Power of Expectancy

Expectations influence perceptions and behaviors in profound
ways. When you expect positive outcomes, you are more likely
to engage in behaviors that support those outcomes. Similarly,
positive expectations can inspire and motivate others, fostering
a productive and cooperative environment. This phenomenon
is supported by psychological principles such as the
Pygmalion effect, where higher expectations lead to improved
performance.

Key Benefits of Positive Expectancy

1. **Enhanced Performance**: Positive expectations can boost
   confidence and motivation, leading to better performance
   and outcomes.

2. **Improved Relationships**: Expecting the best in others can
   enhance interactions and relationships, promoting trust and
   cooperation.

3. **Increased Resilience**: Optimistic expectations can enhance resilience, helping individuals and teams to persevere through challenges and setbacks.

Strategies for Leveraging the Law of Expectancy

1. **Set Clear, Positive Goals**: Define clear and achievable goals with a positive outlook. Visualizing success can help align actions and attitudes toward achieving these goals.

2. **Communicate Optimistically**: Use positive language and affirmations when communicating with others. This can foster a positive atmosphere and encourage others to adopt a similar outlook.

3. **Model Positive Behavior**: Demonstrate positive expectations through your actions and attitudes. Being a role model for optimism can inspire and influence others to follow suit.

4. **Encourage and Support Others**: Recognize and reinforce the potential in others. Providing encouragement and support can help them meet and exceed expectations.

5. **Focus on Solutions**: When faced with challenges, maintain a solution-oriented mindset. Expecting positive outcomes can drive creative problem-solving and innovation.

Applications Across Various Fields

- **Leadership and Management**: Leaders who maintain positive expectations can inspire their teams to achieve higher levels of performance and foster a culture of optimism and resilience.

- **Education**: Teachers with high expectations for their students can positively influence student achievement and engagement.

- **Sales and Marketing**: Sales professionals who expect positive outcomes are more likely to approach clients with confidence and enthusiasm, improving their success rates.

- **Personal Development**: Individuals who adopt a positive expectancy mindset can enhance their personal growth, motivation, and overall well-being.

Ethical Considerations

While maintaining positive expectations is powerful, it is important to remain realistic and grounded. Overly unrealistic expectations can lead to disappointment and disillusionment. Balance optimism with practicality to ensure that expectations are achievable and aligned with actual capabilities and circumstances.

Conclusion

The Law of Expectancy highlights the transformative power of positive anticipation in shaping outcomes. By operating with optimistic expectations, you can influence your own behaviors and attitudes, as well as those of others, creating a self-fulfilling prophecy that drives success. Embracing positive expectancy fosters a productive and cooperative environment, enhances performance, and promotes resilience, making it a vital principle for effective influence and leadership.

CONCLUSION

Harnessing the Power of Influence

The journey through "The 48 Laws of Influence: Mastering the Art of Persuasion" has illuminated various strategic principles that can significantly enhance your ability to influence and persuade others. Each law provides a unique insight into human behavior and the dynamics of effective communication, offering practical techniques to master the art of persuasion.

Integrating the Laws for Comprehensive Influence

While each law stands on its own, the true power of influence comes from integrating these principles into a cohesive approach. Understanding and applying these laws in combination can create a synergistic effect, amplifying your persuasive capabilities and enabling you to navigate complex interpersonal and professional landscapes with greater ease and effectiveness.

Building Trust and Credibility

Many of the laws emphasize the importance of building trust and credibility. Whether through transparency, consistency, or attention to detail, establishing a foundation of trust is crucial for any persuasive effort. People are more likely to be influenced by those they trust and respect, making credibility a cornerstone of effective influence.

Embracing Ethical Persuasion

Throughout this book, the ethical considerations of each law have been highlighted. Ethical persuasion is about enhancing mutual benefit, fostering genuine connections, and promoting positive outcomes. It's essential to approach influence with integrity, ensuring that your efforts are aligned with ethical standards and respect for others.

Adaptability and Continuous Learning

The landscape of influence is dynamic, and the most effective persuaders are those who can adapt to changing circumstances and continuously refine their skills. By staying informed about new techniques, seeking feedback, and learning from each interaction, you can keep your persuasive strategies relevant and impactful.

Empowering Others

True influence is not just about achieving your own goals but also about empowering others to reach theirs. Many of the laws focus on creating win-win scenarios, building collaborative relationships, and fostering environments where everyone can thrive. By empowering others, you enhance your own influence and create a legacy of positive impact.

Final Thoughts

Mastering the art of persuasion is a lifelong journey. The laws outlined in this book provide a robust framework for developing your influence skills, but their application will vary depending on context, personality, and goals. Approach each interaction with curiosity, empathy, and a commitment to ethical influence, and you will find that your ability to persuade and lead will grow exponentially.

As you move forward, remember that influence is both an art and a science. It requires a deep understanding of human nature, strategic thinking, and genuine care for the people you seek to influence. By harnessing the power of these 48 laws, you can master the art of persuasion and become a more effective, ethical, and impactful leader.

GLOSSARY

Acknowledgment: Recognizing and appreciating others' contributions or feelings to build goodwill and trust.

Anchoring: The cognitive bias where an individual relies too heavily on an initial piece of information (the "anchor") when making decisions.

Authority: Establishing credibility and expertise to enhance persuasive efforts.

Balance: Using both emotional and logical appeals to engage different types of audiences effectively.

Cognitive Dissonance: The mental discomfort experienced by a person who holds contradictory beliefs, values, or attitudes, especially relating to behavioral decisions and attitude change.

Commitment: Securing small initial commitments that lead to bigger actions, illustrating the principles of consistency and commitment.

Comparison: The method of evaluating options based on contrasts, setting the right comparative standards to influence decisions.

Consistency: Aligning requests with existing beliefs and behaviors to facilitate compliance and acceptance.

Curiosity: Techniques for sparking and maintaining interest and curiosity, keeping people engaged.

Demonstration: Showing rather than just telling to convince others of the value of an idea, product, or service.

Details: Emphasizing attention to detail to establish credibility and enhance persuasive effectiveness.

Emotional Appeal: Engaging emotions to enhance the impact of a message and influence decision-making.

Expectancy: Operating with positive expectations to shape outcomes through optimistic anticipation.

Exposure: Increasing familiarity through repeated exposure to build comfort and trust, aiding persuasion.

Frequency: The importance of message repetition to ensure it is remembered and acted upon.

Investment: How the effort and resources people invest can increase their commitment and value perception.

Liking: The principle that people are more likely to be influenced by those they like and how personal relationships can affect decisions.

Limitation: How limiting options can help streamline decision-making processes and guide choices more effectively.

Mystery: Using mystery and intrigue to maintain interest and engagement, enhancing the allure of messages or offers.

Novelty: Capturing attention with new and novel ideas to foster greater interest and enthusiasm.

Pain and Pleasure: Behavioral drivers of seeking pleasure and avoiding pain, and how these can be leveraged in persuasive messaging.

Patience: How influence and relationships can grow over time, emphasizing the value of long-term strategies in persuasion.

Power: Projecting strength and certainty to influence perceptions and outcomes.

Reasoning: Using logical, reasoned arguments to support persuasive efforts and influence decisions.

Reciprocity: Giving something first to motivate others to reciprocate, fostering mutual benefit and cooperation.

Reputation: Building and maintaining a reputation to influence interactions and negotiations.

Safety: Providing a sense of safety and reassurance to make messages and propositions more appealing.

Scarcity: The perception of scarcity and how it increases an item's value, making it more desirable.

Silence: How sometimes saying less can be more influential, using strategic silence to enhance the impact of messages.

Social Proof: How individuals look to the behavior and actions of others to determine their own, particularly when they are uncertain.

Stories: The power of storytelling in making messages memorable and engaging, providing a deeper connection with the audience.

Tension: Maintaining a dynamic tension to motivate actions and decisions.

Testimonials: How endorsements from credible sources can lend authority and credibility, enhancing persuasive efforts.

Timing: The importance of timing in persuasion, including how to identify and capitalize on the right moments for maximum impact.

Transparency: The role of openness and honesty in building trust and facilitating influence.

Unity: Creating a sense of belonging and shared identity to enhance the persuasive appeal of ideas and movements.

Urgency: Creating a sense of urgency to prompt immediate action and commitment.

Value: Always offering clear, tangible value in persuasive efforts.

Visibility: The importance of being frequently seen in positive contexts to establish presence and influence.

MOTIVATION

Congratulations on reaching the end of "The 48 Laws of Influence: Mastering the Art of Persuasion and Power." Your dedication to improving your influence and persuasion skills is commendable, and we hope this book has provided you with valuable insights and practical strategies to enhance your personal and professional life.

As you move forward, remember that the true power of influence lies not in manipulation but in the ability to connect with others, inspire positive change, and foster genuine relationships. The principles you've learned are tools to help you navigate complex interactions with integrity and confidence.

Don't be afraid to put these laws into practice. Experiment with different approaches, learn from your experiences, and continue refining your skills. Influence is an ongoing journey of growth and adaptation.

Embrace each opportunity to lead, persuade, and connect with others. Your efforts can make a profound impact on your community, workplace, and personal relationships. By applying these principles ethically and thoughtfully, you can become a force for positive change in the world.

Thank you for embarking on this journey with us. We encourage you to keep learning, stay curious, and always strive to make a difference.

Best of luck on your path to becoming a master of influence. Your journey has only just begun.

With gratitude and encouragement,

Norris Elliott

QUIZ AND ANSWER SECTION

Test your understanding of "The 48 Laws of Influence: Mastering the Art of Persuasion and Power" with this quiz. Reflect on the principles and see how well you can apply them.

Quiz

1. **The Law of Reciprocity**: What is the primary principle behind the Law of Reciprocity? a) To give something to get something in return b) To demand immediate compliance c) To avoid giving anything away d) To ensure maximum profit

2. **The Law of Commitment**: Why is securing small initial commitments effective in persuasion? a) It guarantees a sale b) It leads to bigger actions due to consistency principles c) It eliminates competition d) It saves time

3. **The Law of Social Proof**: How does the Law of Social Proof influence decisions? a) By establishing authority b) By using logical arguments c) By demonstrating that others approve or follow the same behavior d) By creating urgency

4. **The Law of Scarcity**: What effect does emphasizing scarcity have on an item's value? a) Decreases its appeal b) Increases its perceived value and desirability c) Makes it irrelevant d) Ensures it's available to everyone

5. **The Law of Consistency**: How can aligning requests with existing beliefs facilitate compliance? a) By confusing the audience b) By ensuring immediate acceptance c) By aligning with the audience's pre-existing beliefs and behaviors d) By guaranteeing financial gain

6. **The Law of Authority**: How does establishing credibility and expertise enhance persuasive efforts? a) It makes the message longer b) It ensures everyone agrees c) It builds trust and makes the audience more likely to accept the message d) It eliminates all objections

7. **The Law of Novelty**: Why do new and novel ideas capture more attention? a) They are familiar b) They are unexpected and stimulate curiosity c) They are simple d) They are rare

8. **The Law of Transparency**: What is the role of openness and honesty in building trust? a) It confuses the audience b) It hides the real intentions c) It fosters deeper connections and trust d) It ensures immediate compliance

9. **The Law of Urgency**: How does creating a sense of urgency prompt immediate action? a) By relaxing the audience b) By increasing the perceived importance and need to act quickly c) By providing more options d) By eliminating choice

10. **The Law of Value**: Why is it important to always offer clear, tangible value in persuasive efforts? a) To increase length of communication b) To build trust and make the proposition more appealing c) To confuse competitors d) To ensure higher costs

Answers

1. **a)** To give something to get something in return

2. **b)** It leads to bigger actions due to consistency principles

3. **c)** By demonstrating that others approve or follow the same behavior

4. **b)** Increases its perceived value and desirability

5. **c)** By aligning with the audience's pre-existing beliefs and behaviors

6. **c)** It builds trust and makes the audience more likely to accept the message

7. **b)** They are unexpected and stimulate curiosity

8. **c)** It fosters deeper connections and trust

9. **b)** By increasing the perceived importance and need to act quickly

10. **b)** To build trust and make the proposition more appealing

Reflect on your answers and consider how you can apply these laws in your daily interactions and professional endeavors. Mastery of influence is an ongoing journey, and understanding these principles is a significant step towards becoming a more effective and ethical persuader.

BOOKS BY THIS AUTHOR

THE POWER OF NOW: CONQUERING PROCRASTINATION

"The Power of Now: Conquering Procrastination" offers a comprehensive guide to overcoming procrastination. Written by Norris Elliott, a seasoned expert on productivity, this book is a must-read for anyone looking to achieve success and reach their full potential. Drawing from years of experience and a passion for helping others, Norris shares their insights and strategies for time management and overcoming procrastination. With practical tips and actionable advice, this book will help readers conquer their procrastination habits and unlock their full potential. Whether you're a busy professional or a student, "The Power of Now: Conquering Procrastination" will help you take control of your time, increase your productivity, and achieve your goals. Order your copy today and start your journey to a more productive, successful life.

OPEN YOUR BUSINESS: A STEP-BY-STEP GUIDE TO STARTING AND GROWING A

SUCCESSFUL ENTERPRISE

"Open Your Business" is the ultimate guide for aspiring entrepreneurs looking to start and grow their own businesses. Written by an expert in the field, this handbook is packed with practical tips, strategies, and real-world examples that will help you navigate the complex world of business ownership. From developing a business plan and securing funding to attracting and retaining staff and increasing productivity, this book covers all the essential topics you need to know to succeed. With case studies, quizzes, and a step-by-step guide, this book is the perfect tool for anyone looking to turn their business dream into reality. Whether you're just starting out or looking to take your business to the next level, "Open Your Business" is the ultimate guide to success.

WEALTH BY DESIGN: HOW TO BUILD A LIFE OF FINANCIAL FREEDOM

"Financial Literacy and Wealth Building: A Comprehensive Guide" is essential for anyone looking to take control of their financial future. Written by author Ellionaire, this book covers everything you need to know about building wealth and achieving financial freedom, including understanding financial basics, creating a budget, investing, and planning for the future. With real-world examples and practical tips, this book is a must-have for anyone looking to improve their financial literacy and achieve financial success. Whether a beginner or an experienced investor, this book will provide you with the knowledge and tools you need to reach your financial goals. With easy-to-understand language and a step-by-step approach, "Financial Literacy and Wealth Building" is the perfect guide for anyone looking to take control of their finances and build a better future.

THE ASTROLOGY OF LOVE: FIND YOUR PERFECT COMPATIBLE SOUL MATE

Discover the secrets to finding your perfect match with "The Astrology of Love: Find Your Perfect Compatible Soulmate." This enlightening book by celebrated author Norris Elliott offers a unique blend of astrological wisdom and practical advice to guide you on your journey of love and compatibility.

Key Features:

Unlock Love's Cosmic Code: Explore how astrology can influence and guide your romantic journey, helping you find and nurture fulfilling relationships.

Zodiac Compatibility Decoded: Dive deep into the dynamics of each zodiac sign and learn how they interact in love, unveiling the path to your ideal partner.

Planetary Influences Unveiled: Understand how Venus, Mars, and the Moon shape your romantic desires, emotional needs, and relationship styles.

Real-Life Love Stories: Be inspired by real-life examples and case studies that illustrate how astrology has helped others find and sustain love.

Easy-to-Use Astrological Tools: Gain practical and easy-to-apply tools to harness the power of astrology in finding and deepening your romantic connections.

Stunning Visuals and Charts: Enjoy beautifully crafted illustrations and charts that make learning astrology both enjoyable and visually engaging.

Expert Guidance: Benefit from Norris Elliott's extensive research in astrology and relationship counseling, offering insights that are both profound and accessible.

Perfect for:

Singles searching for a meaningful and lasting relationship.
Couples seeking to deepen their understanding and connection.
Astrology enthusiasts eager to explore the romantic aspects of the zodiac.
Readers looking for a blend of entertainment, practical advice, and astrological insight.

Let "The Astrology of Love: Find Your Perfect Compatible Soulmate" be your guide in the journey of love, helping you navigate the stars to find the heart that beats in harmony with yours.

THE POWER OF THE EARTH: EARTH MEDICINE: THE HEALING POWER OF GROUNDING FOR MIND, BODY, AND SOUL

Grounding or earthing is a fascinating and natural practice involving direct physical contact with the Earth's surface. This comprehensive and engaging book explores the latest scientific research and real-world case studies to delve into the potential benefits of grounding for overall health and well-being.

From the antioxidant effect of the Earth's natural supply of electrons to the potential benefits of grounding for improved sleep, reduced pain, stress, and anxiety levels, improved cardiovascular health, and enhanced athletic performance, this book covers all aspects of grounding.

We also explore the spiritual and metaphysical dimensions of grounding, its connection to traditional healing practices and spiritual traditions worldwide, and its potential for personal growth, self-discovery, and spiritual development.

The book also discusses practical tips for helping children incorporate grounding into their daily routines, the connection between grounding and our relationship with nature, and the potential for grounding to mitigate the harmful effects of environmental toxins on the body.

In the final chapter, we explore the potential for grounding to become a mainstream health practice and the potential for new technologies and innovations to enhance the practice of grounding.

Overall, this book offers a compelling and comprehensive guide to the fascinating practice of grounding and its potential to improve overall health and well-being naturally and holistically.

JAMAICANISM: THE HEARTBEAT OF THE ISLAND

"Jamaicanism: The Heartbeat of the Island" - Discover Jamaica Like Never Before

Embark on an enthralling journey with "Jamaicanism: The Heartbeat of the Island," a book that peels back the layers of a land pulsating with life, culture, and history. This is not just a read; it's an experience that transports you to the vibrant heart of Jamaica. Feel the rhythm of the island through every page, as you uncover the essence of Jamaicanism.

Why "Jamaicanism" is a Must-Read:

Dive into the Rich Tapestry of Jamaican Culture: Explore the depths of Jamaican culture, from the soul-stirring beats of reggae to the vibrant traditions of dancehall. This book celebrates the diverse heritage that shapes the Jamaican spirit.

Uncover a Lush Historical Landscape: Journey through Jamaica's past, from the indigenous Taino people to the triumphs of independence. Witness the resilience of a nation shaped by a complex history of colonization and liberation.

Speak the Language of the Island: Delve into the world of Jamaican Patois, a language born from a melting pot of influences, encapsulating the island's unique cultural identity and history.

Savor the Flavors of Jamaican Cuisine: Embark on a culinary adventure with the tantalizing tastes of Jamaica. From spicy jerk chicken to sweet ackee and saltfish, discover recipes and stories behind the island's famous dishes.

Meet the People Who Shape Jamaica: Hear the stories of Jamaicans who've left their mark on the world. From iconic figures like Bob Marley and Usain Bolt to the everyday heroes shaping Jamaica's future.

Explore the Natural Beauty of Jamaica: From the misty Blue Mountains to the crystal-clear waters of the Caribbean Sea, experience the breathtaking landscapes that make Jamaica a paradise on earth.

Witness the Power of Social Change: Understand the contemporary challenges facing Jamaica and the inspiring initiatives driving social progress, environmental stewardship, and economic growth.

Experience the Vibrant Jamaican Festivals: Immerse yourself in the pulsating energy of Jamaican festivals, where music, dance, and heritage come alive in a spectacular display of cultural pride.

"Jamaicanism: The Heartbeat of the Island" is more than a book; it's a celebration of an island and its people. It's a journey that will captivate, educate, and inspire. Whether you're a seasoned traveler, a cultural enthusiast, or simply a lover of compelling stories, this book is your gateway to experiencing the true spirit of Jamaica.

Grab your copy today and let the rhythms of Jamaica move you!

PUTTING DOWN THE BULLY: FINALLY!

"Bullying is a pervasive problem that affects individuals of all ages and can devastate mental and physical health. In "Standing Up Against Bullying," "Putting Down The Bully" examines the various forms of bullying and its impacts. Through practical tips and coping strategies, readers will learn how to deal with bullying, seek help and support, and take action to overcome bullying. The author also highlights the role of bystanders and the importance of speaking up and taking a stand. With personal stories from those who have overcome bullying and a focus on hope and resilience, this book offers a comprehensive guide for anyone looking to make a difference and reclaim a sense of control and empowerment."

EMPOWERING WOMEN:

OVERCOMING MARGINALIZATION

This book comprehensively examines women's marginalization, exploring the root causes and how media, technology, globalization, economic policies, governments, civil society, men and boys, and data and research all play a role. The author, who has a construction engineering and management background, wrote this book responding to a friend's fear of publishing her similar study on the topic. Through insightful analysis and real-world examples, this book offers a call to action for continued progress toward gender equality and eliminating women's marginalization—a must-read for anyone seeking to understand the complex issues facing women worldwide today.

HOW TO BE HAPPY: THE SECRET TO FINDING HAPPINESS

Looking for a guide to cultivating happiness and finding meaning in life? Look no further than this insightful and inspiring book! Drawing on the latest scientific research, personal stories and experiences, and practical tips and techniques, this book will help you cultivate happiness and find fulfillment in all aspects of your life. Whether you are looking to improve your relationships, find success and meaning at work, or simply find peace and contentment, this book will provide you with the tools and guidance you need to achieve your goals. So why wait? Start your journey to happiness and fulfillment today!

THE CONFIDENT MAN: THE ART OF

SELF-ASSURANCE AND MAGNETISM

The Confident Man: The Art of Self-Assurance and Magnetism is a comprehensive guide to help men develop a confident and charismatic persona. Through insightful theory and practical exercises, the author provides readers with the tools and techniques needed to build self-confidence and improve their communication skills. This book is written by Norris Elliott, an expert in the field of self-improvement and personal development. The book covers critical topics such as developing a solid mindset, enhancing body language, improving communication skills, building self-awareness, and putting it all together. With real-world case studies, personal anecdotes, and expert insights, this book offers a unique and practical approach to self-assurance and magnetism. Whether you're looking to improve your personal or professional life, The Confident Man is the perfect guide to help you achieve your goals. So why wait? Start your journey to becoming a confident and charismatic man today!.

With clear, concise instructions and practical advice, "My Perfect Wedding" will help you plan a wedding that reflects your style and unique vision. Whether starting from scratch or just needing inspiration, this book is a must-have for every bride-to-be."

This comprehensive guide offers everything you need to plan your perfect wedding from start to finish.

LOVE TRIANGLE: THE PERFECT PLAN. A ROMANTIC COMEDY.

Emma had always been a type-A planner. She was the kind of

kid who color-coded her crayon box and had a five-year plan for her Barbies. As an adult, she turned her love for organization into a successful event-planning business. She was like a human version of Google Calendar - always on top of everyone's schedule and ensuring every detail was in its place.

Emma's latest project was her own wedding. She had meticulously planned every detail, from the seating chart to the number of sprinkles on the cake. She even had a backup plan for the backup plan. This was going to be the perfect wedding, damn it.

Enter Olivia, Emma's business partner and the Robin to her Batman. Olivia had some big news - she was pregnant and wouldn't be able to help with the wedding. Emma's reaction was somewhere between "Oh my god, congratulations!" and "Oh my god, what are we going to do?!"

As Emma was having a meltdown, an old friend named Max called. He was in town for a wedding but had missed his flight and needed a place to crash. Emma reluctantly agreed to let him stay with her, hoping he wouldn't mess up her perfectly planned life.

Max was like a walking hurricane. He was spontaneous, carefree, and the kind of guy who would jump out of a plane without checking to see if his parachute was attached. Emma was equal parts fascinated and terrified by him.

THE BAKING BOOK: CAKES, PIES, TARTS, BREAD, PUDDINGS, BARS, AND COOKIES, COOKING

The Baking Book; Cakes, Pies, Tarts, Bread, Puddings, bars, and Cookies, Cooking is the ultimate guide to help you master the art of baking. This comprehensive book covers everything from cakes, pastries, and pies to loaves of bread and puddings. You'll learn about essential baking equipment, ingredients, schedules, conversions, and history. Whether you're a novice or an experienced baker, this book is packed with tips and tricks, troubleshooting guides, and much more. Discover the science behind baking and how to perfect your techniques for consistent results every time. With easy-to-follow recipes and step-by-step instructions, you'll be able to create delicious baked goods that everyone will love. So why wait? Start baking with confidence and make it happen with The Baking Book. Baking, Cakes, Pastries, Pies, Bread, Puddings, Baking Equipment, Ingredients, Baking Schedules, Conversions, History, Tips, Tricks, and Troubleshooting.

SEDUCER: THE ART OF SEDUCTION

Unleash the Art of Seduction with this comprehensive guide! Discover the secrets of captivating and satisfying relationships through a blend of mindfulness, cultural awareness, and sexual technique. This book guides you on a journey of self-discovery, helping you develop a more intentional approach to your relationships and interactions. With tips and advice for navigating every stage of a relationship, this book is a must-read for anyone looking to spice up their love life. Get your copy today and start your seductive journey!

BE A CONFIDENT WOMAN: HOW TO GAIN CONFIDENCE

If you want to boost your self-confidence, improve your communication skills, and build a more charismatic persona, then Be A Confident Woman: How To Gain Confidence is the perfect book for you. Written by an expert in self-improvement and personal development, this book offers a comprehensive guide to help you achieve your personal and professional goals.

BE A CONFIDENT MAN: HOW TO GAIN CONFIDENCE

Through insightful theory and practical exercises, you'll learn the tools and techniques needed to develop a solid mindset, enhance your body language, improve your communication skills, build self-awareness, and put it all together. The real-world case studies, personal anecdotes, and expert insights in this book provide a unique and practical approach to self-assurance and magnetism.

Whether you're looking to advance your career, build stronger relationships, or simply feel more confident in your daily life, The Confident Man has something to offer. So, if you're ready to start your journey towards becoming a confident and charismatic man, then this book is a must-have!

THE 3 6 9 METHOD OF MANIFESTATION: PERSONALIZED PATHS TO SUCCESS THROUGH ANCIENT WISDOM

Unlock the Secret Power of the Universe with THE 3 6 9 METHOD OF MANIFESTATION: Personalized Paths to Success Through Ancient Wisdom

◻ Discover the transformative power of Nikola Tesla's secret code —Learn how the numbers 3, 6, and 9 can unlock your potential to manifest desires.

◻ Master the Art of Manifestation—Step-by-step guidance on integrating the 3 6 9 method into your daily routine for effective manifestation.

◻ Tailor the Practice to Your Life—Personalization techniques to ensure the 3 6 9 method resonates with your unique energy and lifestyle.

◻ Navigate Life's Challenges—Practical solutions for overcoming skepticism, obstacles, and maintaining your commitment to your manifestation journey.

◻ Real Success Stories—Be inspired by real-life examples of individuals who have successfully used the 3 6 9 method to change their lives.

◻ Comprehensive FAQs and Resources—Your burning questions are answered, plus resources for further exploration and deepening your practice.

Whether you're a seasoned practitioner of the law of attraction or new to the concept of manifestation, this book offers a fresh perspective on how to harness universal energies to create the life you've always dreamed of. Dive deep into the mystery and mechanics of the 3 6 9 method, and embark on a journey of self-discovery, personal growth, and unimaginable success.

Start manifesting your desires with clarity, purpose, and a

newfound understanding of the universe's profound wisdom. Your journey to a more fulfilled life begins here.

THE LIVE SOCIAL MEDIA STREAMING BIBLE: HOW TO DOMINATE THE LIVE STREAMING WORLD: A SIMPLE GET TO THE POINT GUIDE TO MAKE YOU FAMOUS AND RICH

"Unleash the power of live streaming with 'THE LIVE SOCIAL MEDIA STREAMING BIBLE.' This comprehensive guide is your key to building a successful career in the digital age. From setting up your stream to engaging your audience, monetizing your content to navigating legal and ethical considerations, this book covers it all. With practical tips, expert insights, and real-life case studies, you'll learn how to create compelling content, grow your audience, and turn your passion into a profitable career. Whether you're a seasoned streamer or just starting, 'THE LIVE SOCIAL MEDIA STREAMING BIBLE' is your ultimate resource for success in the world of live streaming. Get your copy today and take your streaming game to the next level!"

- [ ] Setting up your stream
- [ ] Engaging your audience
- [ ] Monetizing your content
- [ ] Navigating legal and ethical considerations
- [ ] Practical tips and expert insights
- [ ] Real-life case studies

- [ ] Creating compelling content
- [ ] Growing your audience
- [ ] Turning your passion into a profitable career
- [ ] Ultimate resource for success in the world of live-streaming

BBL: EVERYTHING YOU SHOULD KNOW BEFORE, DURING AND AFTER

Embark on a transformative journey with "Brazilian Butt Lifts Everything You Should Know Before, During and After" and unlock the secrets to achieving your dream silhouette!

☐ Comprehensive Insights: Dive into a wealth of knowledge, from pre-surgery considerations to post-op care, all crafted by top industry experts.

☐ Real-Life Transformations: Be inspired by genuine stories, rich in detail and emotion, guiding you through real experiences.

☐ Safety as Priority: Navigate the complexities of cosmetic procedures with our in-depth safety guides and surgeon selection tips.

☐ Innovation at Your Fingertips: Stay ahead with the latest trends and technological advancements in the field.

Elevate your journey from aspiration to reality. This guide isn't just a book; it's your partner in achieving the confidence and curves you've always desired!

THE ASTROLOGY IN OUR

PERSONALITIES: A MASTER COMPILATION OF THE 12 BOOKS OF THE ZODIAC SIGNS THAT MAKES US WHO WE ARE. EVERY SIGN HOLDS THE KEY TO UNLOCKING ... WONDERS OF THE UNIVERSE & IN US

"The Astrology in Our Personalities: A Master Compilation of the 12 Books of the Zodiac Signs That Makes Us Who We Are" is an essential addition to your library, offering a unique and comprehensive exploration of the zodiac and its impact on our lives. Here's why you should buy this book:

Deep Understanding of Each Zodiac Sign: Uncover the traits, strengths, and challenges unique to each sign, offering a deeper understanding of yourself and those around you.

Personal Growth and Self-Discovery: Navigate through the insights provided for each sign to embark on a journey of self-discovery, helping you to unlock your potential and embrace your true self.

Improve Relationships: By understanding the astrological influences on personalities, foster stronger, more empathetic connections with friends, family, and partners.

Comprehensive Astrological Guide: From Aries to Pisces, this master compilation brings together extensive knowledge about all 12 zodiac signs, making it a one-stop resource for anyone interested in astrology.

Celestial Guidance for Life's Journey: Gain celestial insights into decision-making, personal development, and life's challenges, using the wisdom of the stars as a guiding light.

Beautifully Crafted Narratives: Each section is crafted with care, combining astrological wisdom with engaging narratives that make complex concepts accessible and enjoyable to read.

Cultural and Historical Insights: Delve into the fascinating cultural and historical contexts of astrology, enriching your understanding of its timeless relevance and influence.

Empowerment Through the Stars: Discover how the alignment of the stars at your birth influences your personality and life path, empowering you with the knowledge to navigate life more confidently.

Ideal for Both Beginners and Enthusiasts: Whether you're new to astrology or a seasoned enthusiast, this book provides valuable insights that will deepen your understanding and appreciation of the zodiac.

Perfect Gift for the Astrology Lover: With its comprehensive coverage and insightful exploration of the zodiac, this book is the perfect gift for anyone with an interest in astrology and the mysteries of the cosmos.

Embark on a celestial journey of exploration, self-discovery, and enlightenment with "The Astrology in Our Personalities." Unlock the mysteries of the universe and the wonders within yourself, guided by the timeless wisdom of the stars.

LEARN HOW TO SAY NO WITHOUT FEELING GUILTY: RECLAIM YOUR TIME, SPACE, POWER AND BUILD THE LIFE YOU DESERVE

Book Description: "Learn How to Say No Without Feeling Guilty: Reclaim Your Time, Space, Power and Build the Life You Deserve" In a world brimming with opportunities and demands, the ability to set boundaries and prioritize one's own needs is more crucial than ever. "Learn How to Say No Without Feeling Guilty" offers a comprehensive guide to mastering the art of refusal, empowering readers to reclaim control over their lives and embark on a journey towards personal fulfillment and well-being.

Why is this book a must-have on your shelf? Let's check the boxes:

Reclaim Your Time: Uncover strategies to manage your time effectively, freeing yourself from the clutches of overcommitment and opening up space for pursuits that truly matter to you.

Cultivate Personal Space: Learn the importance of protecting your emotional and physical space by setting healthy boundaries that honor your well-being and facilitate personal growth.

Empower Yourself: Gain the confidence to stand firm in your decisions, empower yourself by saying no without the burden of guilt, and take charge of your life's direction.

Build the Life You Deserve: Step by step, learn to prioritize your dreams, needs, and happiness to build a life that reflects your true values and aspirations.

Navigate Complex Relationships: Discover tactful ways to assert your boundaries within personal and professional relationships without damaging connections or causing unnecessary conflict.

Transform Guilt into Gratitude: Shift your perspective from feeling guilty about saying no to embracing gratitude for the opportunity to align your actions with your true self.

Access to Exclusive Resources: Benefit from QR-coded links to exclusive online resources, including workshops, personal assessments, and a supportive community forum to aid your journey.

"Learn How to Say No Without Feeling Guilty" is not just another self-help book; it's a lifeline for those who feel stretched thin, undervalued, or misunderstood. Through heartfelt advice, actionable strategies, and real-life examples, this book guides you towards a liberating path of self-discovery and empowerment.

Whether you're struggling to balance professional obligations, navigating challenging personal relationships, or simply seeking to cultivate a more mindful and intentional lifestyle, this book holds the key to unlocking your full potential.

Invest in your well-being, harness the power of no, and start building the life you truly deserve today.

EPILOGUE

The Ongoing Journey of Influence

As you close this book, remember that the art of influence is a continuous journey, not a final destination. The principles and strategies outlined in "The 48 Laws of Influence: Mastering the Art of Persuasion and Power" are tools to be honed and adapted over time, aligning with your evolving experiences and goals. Influence is dynamic, requiring ongoing learning, practice, and refinement.

Reflecting on Your Path

Take a moment to reflect on your personal journey with influence. Consider how far you've come and the areas where you've seen growth. Recognize your successes and identify opportunities for further development. The knowledge you've gained here is a foundation upon which you can build, continuously enhancing your ability to connect with, persuade, and inspire others.

Embracing Adaptability and Flexibility

The world around us is constantly changing, and so too are the contexts in which we seek to influence. Flexibility and adaptability are essential qualities for any effective persuader. Be open to new ideas, stay informed about emerging trends, and be willing to adjust your strategies as needed. This adaptability will ensure that your influence remains relevant and effective in any situation.

Cultivating Empathy and Authenticity

At the heart of effective influence lies a deep understanding of and respect for others. Cultivating empathy and authenticity in your interactions not only enhances your ability to persuade but also builds lasting, meaningful relationships. Authentic influence is about connecting on a human level, understanding others' perspectives, and fostering mutual respect and trust.

The Ripple Effect of Positive Influence

Your journey in mastering the art of persuasion has the potential to create a ripple effect, extending far beyond your immediate interactions. By applying these laws ethically and with integrity, you can inspire and empower others, creating a positive impact that spreads through your personal and professional networks. Your influence can be a force for good, driving positive change and fostering environments where everyone can thrive.

Continuing the Legacy

As you move forward, consider how you can contribute to the broader conversation about influence and leadership. Share your experiences, mentor others, and continue to learn from those around you. By passing on your knowledge and insights, you help to cultivate a new generation of ethical and effective influencers.

A Final Note of Encouragement

Remember, influence is not about manipulating or controlling others; it's about inspiring, guiding, and creating positive outcomes. It's about leading with empathy, integrity, and respect. As you apply the principles from this book, stay true to your values and strive to make a meaningful difference in the lives of those you influence.

Thank you for embarking on this journey of influence and persuasion. May the insights and strategies you've gained empower you to achieve your goals, build stronger relationships, and create a lasting, positive impact in your world. The journey of influence is ongoing, and the possibilities are endless. Continue to grow, learn, and inspire, and let your influence shine.

DISCLAIMER

The information contained in "The 48 Laws of Influence: Mastering the Art of Persuasion and Power" is for educational and informational purposes only. While the author has made every effort to ensure the accuracy and completeness of the content, it is not intended to replace professional advice or to be used as a substitute for specific guidance in personal or professional decision-making.

The strategies and principles outlined in this book are based on the author's research and experiences and may not apply to all situations or individuals. Readers are encouraged to use their judgment and discretion when applying the concepts presented. The author and publisher disclaim any liability or responsibility for any adverse effects or consequences resulting from the use or application of the information contained in this book.

Furthermore, the ethical considerations discussed throughout the book are intended to guide readers in the responsible use of influence. It is essential to practice these principles with integrity, respect for others, and adherence to applicable laws and ethical standards.

By reading this book, you acknowledge that the author and publisher are not responsible for any actions taken based on the content and that the use of the information provided is at your own risk.

DEAR VALUED READER,

Thank you for investing your time in reading this book. I hope it has enriched your understanding and provided practical insights that you can apply in your daily life. If you found value in this book, please consider taking a moment to leave a review.

Your feedback is incredibly important for several reasons:

Support Authors: Reviews can significantly support authors, both by offering constructive feedback and by providing encouragement for their work. Sharing your thoughts helps authors understand what resonated with you and what might be improved in future works.

Guide Other Readers: Your review can help other potential readers make informed decisions. By sharing your experience, you offer insights into what the book offers, helping others determine if it's the right choice for their needs and interests.

Enhance Book Visibility: Reviews contribute to the visibility of a book in online marketplaces. More reviews can improve a book's ranking and visibility, making it more accessible to a wider audience.

Create Community Dialogue: Your opinions contribute to a larger discussion about the themes and topics covered in the book. This can foster a community of like-minded individuals who share interests and recommendations.

I appreciate your time and your thoughts. Leaving a review, whether detailed or brief, makes a difference and is deeply valued.

Thank you once again for your support and for being a vital part of the reading community.

Warm regards,

Norris Elliott

JOIN OUR EMAIL LIST

Dear Reader,

We invite you to join our email list for updates, exclusive content, and special offers. By signing up, you'll receive:

- Notifications about new book releases
- Exclusive insights and tips on influence and persuasion
- Invitations to webinars and events
- Special promotions and discounts

To join our email list, simply send an email to

ellionairebooks@gmail.com with the subject line "Subscribe." We look forward to staying connected and continuing to support your journey in mastering the art of influence.

Thank you for your support!

Warm regards,

[Norris Elliott]
Ellionaire Books

Email: ellionairebooks@gmail.com

NOTES

NOTES

Made in the USA
Columbia, SC
30 June 2024

03012986-489e-44e3-bb62-72efd835b4c0R01